Teleworking: A Good Practice Guide

Madeleine Grinyer
of Knowledge Brokers

Chartered Institute of Housing
and The Housing Corporation

The Chartered Institute of Housing

The Chartered Institute of Housing is the professional organisation for all people who work in housing. Its purpose is to take a strategic and leading role in encouraging and promoting the provision of good quality affordable housing for all. The Institute has more than 15,000 members working in local authorities, housing associations, the private sector and educational institutions.

Chartered Institute of Housing
Octavia House, Westwood Way
Coventry CV4 8JP
Tel: 01203 851700
Fax: 01203 695110

The Housing Corporation

The Housing Corporation is the government agency which registers, regulates and funds over 2,000 social landlords in England, which between them provide around one million homes for people in need. The Corporation has an important role as a promoter of good practice in the social housing sector.

The Housing Corporation
149 Tottenham Court Road
London W1P 0BN
Tel: 0171-393 2000

Teleworking: A Good Practice Guide
Written by Madeleine Grinyer of Knowledge Brokers
Editor: Ross Fraser, Chartered Institute of Housing

Published by the Chartered Institute of Housing
and The Housing Corporation
ISBN: 1 900396 66 1

Design by Jeremy Spencer
Cover illustration by Nina Davis
Printed by Hobbs the Printers, Totton

Contents

FOREWORD

Hundreds of thousands of people in the UK and millions in the USA, employed in a wide range of occupations in different industries, spend at least part of their working hours located away from their offices, using telecommunications technology to keep in touch with customers and staff.

Teleworking means working away from the traditional workplace or office. This can be either at home, in-transit or on other people's premises, and involves communicating with the rest of the organisation using the appropriate hardware and software linked by telecommunications. This Guide introduces new ways of working which can not only help the social housing sector deliver services better and more cost effectively, but also radically restructure organisations.

The potential advantages of teleworking to organisations in terms of cost savings and improved customer service could be significant, depending upon their individual circumstances. There can also be potential benefits to employees through empowerment, better use of time and increased job satisfaction.

The social housing sector has often been slow in seizing on the potential benefits which technology can bring. As we move into the new millennium, however, it is clear that registered social landlords (RSLs), local authorities and other social housing providers could gain significantly from adopting teleworking and other solutions to the perennial problem of meeting increased demand with fewer resources.

The Guide looks at the pressures for change in ways of working in social housing, including the need to cut costs, improve service and efficiency and attract and retain good staff.

The Guide sets out current developments in housing and the related use of new technologies. It describes the recent progress in telecommunications, which has produced such concepts as 'virtual offices', 'teleworking' and 'flexible office space'. In particular, the Guide explores the potential for 'teleworking' and related ways of working in the social housing field.

Some of these new concepts could be and are being introduced by RSLs and other providers of social housing, but the pace of change could be faster. If housing organisations miss this opportunity, they may find themselves facing the new millennium with increasingly outdated equipment and cumbersome ways of working.

The Guide provides advice on how to introduce change, identifying the barriers to change and the practical steps which should be taken to overcome them. It also highlights how to ensure that staff and customers are kept informed and involved in changes.

The Guide cannot cover all issues in depth nor address each organisation's specific needs. Social housing providers seeking to take up the ideas in this Guide will need to seek further, specialist advice.

Roger Jarman
Head of Housing Management
The Housing Corporation

Ross Fraser
Director of Professional Practice
Chartered Institute of Housing

May 1999

About the Author

Knowledge Brokers was formed in 1994 and is one of the most successful consultancies specialising in organisational development in the UK. Madeleine Grinyer is the founder and managing director of Knowledge Brokers.

Madeleine Grinyer is an international authority on large-scale business development, having written and presented the international best selling BBC video *Benchmarking for Competitive Advantage* and designed a BBC television programme on improving competitive performance and is a sought after conference and business school speaker. She is also recognised as an expert in the human aspects of information technology.

Knowledge Brokers has a wide experience of advising on and implementing remote working practices in order to considerably reduce costs and improve services. This has included redesigning housing management services and particularly customer contact using technologies such as call centres.

Knowledge Brokers' clients include major blue chip businesses plus organisations working in the fields of social housing, utilities and financial services.

Madeleine Grinyer may be contacted at:

Knowledge Brokers
69 King George Square
Richmond
Surrey TW10 6LF

Telephone: 0181-332 0193

Acknowledgements

I would like to thank all those who have kindly helped me to understand in depth the issues in social housing and have taken a personal interest in understanding how this way of working will help the sector. I should particularly like to thank Anthony Mayer, Chief Executive of The Housing Corporation for his interest and support, Roger Jarman, Head of Housing Management at The Housing Corporation, for his sponsorship, and Adrian Moran of The Housing Corporation for his ideas. I would also particularly like to acknowledge Ross Fraser of the Chartered Institute of Housing for his enthusiastic support and to Joanna Jeffrey for her editorial assistance.

I am also grateful to the following registered social landlords who have also helped the study by providing cases studies, responses to our surveys and comments in general:

Bedfordshire Pilgrims
Broomleigh
English Churches
Hexagon
Housing 21
Hyde
Johnnie Johnson
Metropolitan
North British
Northern Counties
Riverside
Sanctuary
Western Challenge

I also wish to express my deepest gratitude to my partner, Davide Ferrara, for his valuable ideas, the support he gives me and for his excellent contribution in the final chapter of this book on the future of social housing.

Madeleine Grinyer
May 1999

Introduction

Registered social landlords (RSLs), local authorities and other social landlords have to meet two, sometimes apparently contradictory, objectives. They are expected to provide a high quality service to their tenants and applicants whilst being expected to reduce costs and keep rents affordable.

For RSLs in particular, there is often conflict between social and commercial objectives. In many instances, people working at the sharp end of the business are aiming to provide a social service, while others in the organisation may be seeking to create surpluses, to be used for investment or diversification.

This Guide examines how new ways of working, made possible by the appropriate use of technology, can help the social housing sector achieve as many of its objectives as possible. In particular it looks at the contribution that 'teleworking' can make to cost effectiveness.

The Guide does not set out a blueprint for new ways of working. Instead, it recognises that each social landlord works with a unique combination of tenants, leaseholders, applicants, stock and staff. However, every social landlord, which is considering changing its working methods to maximise the use of new technologies and flexible working practices, needs to take into account the content of this Guide.

Case study material both from within the social housing sector and from elsewhere is used to illustrate some of the benefits and pitfalls of introducing the new ways of working.

The Guide will interest **all** people working in social housing, their trades union or staff representatives, and their customers.

CHAPTER 1

THE CHANGING CULTURE OF SOCIAL HOUSING

This chapter looks at why registered social landlords (RSLs), local authorities and other social landlords are re-examining how they deliver their services and why they are adopting new ways of working.

In part, these changes reflect the challenges currently facing RSLs and local authority housing departments in the way they deliver housing and associated services. Other pressures come from changes in the wider society within which social housing organisations operate.

❑ 1.1 Pressure on costs

In recent years, RSLs and local authorities have been operating within decreasing levels of funding. There seems little likelihood that this pattern will change. All social landlords, therefore, need to look at how to reduce their running costs. New ways of working are crucial here – it is estimated, for example, that teleworking today is saving £1.5 billion in rent and business rates alone.

❑ 1.2 Demands for better service

Service expectations, both from customers – such as tenants and leaseholders – and from regulators and auditors, are now increasing, particularly in the context of Best Value. Customers are increasingly coming to expect good value service and fast delivery in all areas of their lives, including housing. The development of 24-hour banking and insurance services has created an expectation that service activity should not end at 5 pm on a weekday. Customers who are used to being given exact appointment times when they ask a television repairer to call, expect to be given an equally precise appointment time by a repairs contractor when they report a problem. Customers are becoming used to using new communications and payments technology themselves, whether to buy tickets for the cinema, a football match or find details of train or bus services.

The Housing Corporation's move towards ever more precise and stringent performance indicators and performance standards, and the Government's introduction of Best Value, are further forces driving RSLs and authorities to examine the way they operate. Accurate and real-time monitoring systems are needed to ensure that services are being provided in line with standards and targets.

❑ 1.3 Responsiveness to change

Over the last 20 years there have been significant changes in the roles social landlords are expected to play in providing housing. There have been periods of growth, of reduction, of new funding regimes and changing priorities, such as the current Housing Plus, and Best Value initiatives. Harnessing new technology and flexible ways of working can make social housing organisations better able to react swiftly to changes. Maximising the use of technology to provide quick and accurate information can be invaluable in terms of cost and activity analysis and monitoring the service. Social landlords able to examine critically service cost and quality are also better able to compete for scarce resources.

❑ 1.4 Efficiency and quality

One way in which social landlords and organisations outside housing have responded to competition and pressure for improved, more cost-effective services, has been to focus on meeting customer needs and to seek improvements in customer service. Pursuing quality has led many social landlords to adopt initiatives such as quality circles, focus groups, total quality management, benchmarking and, more recently, business process re-engineering (BPR). Terms such as core business, teamworking and empowerment have all been translated from the commercial and business worlds into the social housing sphere.

Social housing landlords which have worked through these processes are beginning the process of improving their cost base and service levels. They are focusing on delivering good services, which their tenants and leaseholders actually want, more quickly and developing a work culture where people are becoming more used to taking on responsibility for their part in delivering the service.

There has also been a recognition that adopting 'commercial' values and practice need not mean losing 'caring' values – that the commercial skills of cost and customer awareness and a 'results driven' approach to work are welcome in social housing.

Organisations are re-appraising their ways of working to enable them to make leaps in business performance rather than merely match others within their own industry. Social landlords should no longer simply seek to study performance indicator tables and to catch up with the best, or even the average, performance within their sector. They should be looking to set entirely new performance standards which compare with the best organisations irrespective of their industry. New work patterns and new approaches to learning, when effectively deployed, will enhance their ability to deliver substantial performance improvements.

❑ 1.5 Increased computer literacy

Younger people today have grown up in an age of personal computing and take for granted that technology will play an important part in the workplace. They may well have IT skills which they wish to use and develop at work. Elsewhere in society, communications technology awareness is growing fast. Over the last few years many older people have had to become computer literate to do their jobs.

❑ 1.6 Technological development

The costs of technology are falling fast as its capabilities increase. A Pentium PC (personal computer) with multimedia, for example, today costs less than half the price of a Pentium PC without multimedia four years ago. Modems are increasingly sold as standard with PCs; national and international telecommunications are switching to digital systems to improve speed, quality and efficiency. Optical fibres giving broad bandwidths are likely to revolutionise the ability to communicate using comparatively low cost, real-time video globally around the millennium. More detail on the enabling technology which can support new ways of working is given in Chapter 7.

❑ 1.7 Attracting and keeping staff

Recent patterns of high unemployment have encouraged an attitude among some social landlords, as among other employers, that it is a 'buyer's market' when it comes to recruiting staff. Future projections of skill and labour availability suggest, however, that companies will have to compete to attract and retain good staff. Pressure on costs limits the potential for social landlords to attract staff through offering ever higher salaries. However, they **can** build on the commitment and interest of staff and applicants by improving job satisfaction. This can be achieved by helping staff develop their technological skills, providing the hardware and software to let them do their job well and encouraging flexible working practices which may include working from home, working whilst travelling and working when on customers' premises. Many staff working in social housing think that the changes in working practices which have diminished contact with tenants have not always been for the best. Teleworking will go a long way in redressing any such imbalance at the customer interface. Ways of working which enable them to spend more time out of the office, working face-to-face with tenants, will promote greater job satisfaction, provided that the right information and communication processes are in place.

Developing an office culture which values staff skills and encourages teamworking can also engage loyalty. Such a culture depends upon good access to information, excellent communication, and continuous individual and organisational development.

Some people may have physical barriers to overcome in order to travel to work or to work in traditional offices. Technological advances and flexible ways of working can help remove some of these barriers to the employment of disabled people. With the Disability Discrimination Act 1995 now in force, employers should be thinking about ensuring that they do not discriminate in any way against disabled staff, applicants or tenants.

❑ 1.8 Future trends

The world of social housing is constantly changing. The significant increase in competition is hastening the pace of change. In future, RSLs may be involved in mergers or partnerships either with other RSLs or local authorities. They may become involved in developing 'added value' services or move into provision for different needs groups. In each scenario, access to good and quick information and the ability to respond quickly to opportunities is essential. This means changing ways of working.

Chapter 2

The New Information Society

This chapter presents an overview of the new ways of working which organisations are using to harness the benefits of technology and meet future challenges. It introduces concepts such as the 'virtual office' and 'teleworking', and summarises some of the main technological advances which underpin new ways of working.

❑ 2.1 Housing in cyberspace

Imagine the virtual social landlord, a social housing organisation that has freed itself from the problems of geography, expensive city property prices and reliance on a local skills pool.

The chief executive works from her home. Tenants calling the company dial a single freephone number, which is answered by call centre staff working at home in the various geographical centres within which the landlord operates. From there, they can schedule visits by housing officers working in the various 'patches' where the landlord has properties. Appointments for repairs are made directly into the contractors' electronic diaries so that tenants know exactly when the operative will call and best use is made of the operative's time by matching jobs to where people are already working.

The chief executive's personal assistant, shared by three other executives in the organisation, operates from an office in a converted bedroom at his home. He, like all employees, has access via his PC and the telephone system to the company's database, held on servers maintained by an external company somewhere in the M4 corridor. This external company provides an electronic mailing system and holds all the employees' diaries, the data on which housing officers and maintenance staff are working, and an archive of information pertaining to the property and condition of the housing stock.

There is a public relations officer who works from home. She is paid part-time but available full-time to deal, as needed, with public relations and commercial marketing work. The virtual social landlord knows its marketplace intimately and can position itself accurately in terms of the skills it needs and geographical spread.

The housing officers spend most of their time visiting tenants. They are supported by advanced telephone and voice mail systems and laptop computers. When they need to meet each other face-to-face, they use meeting space at the small satellite offices which the landlord rents. Some of these are on housing estates, others are shared with local businesses not in the social housing sector. They communicate daily on an 'as and when' basis via video conferencing via their PCs. Groupware on their computers enables the sharing of files and transferring of tenant and property records. This technology also permits staff to work on business development projects remotely.

Allocations are handled by a member of staff who, because of severe arthritis, finds travelling to work and working from 9 to 5 difficult, but can work at home with frequent breaks. Twice a month she meets other staff face-to-face. The rest of the time she keeps in touch via a video conferencing link.

All the staff keep in touch with each other using e-mail and their groupware. This may sound like science fiction, but it is not. The scenario is feasible. All the elements are taken from case studies of companies operating in the UK today, which have used technology to eliminate the need for high overheads and capital tied up in expensive offices, and for employees to struggle through heavy traffic, late trains and poor weather conditions. They have all, as social landlords need to, looked at themselves without the old familiar limits of place, time and physical resources and redesigned how they operate.

❑ 2.2 The virtual office

The 'virtual office' is defined by Organisation and Technology Research (OTR) as "the name given to the set of facilities that enables a person to carry out his or her job regardless of location."

An effective virtual office has two main elements:

- portable equipment for staff, enabling them to communicate easily with each other and with any corporate databases wherever they are; and
- very few fixed offices – which are mainly used for meeting specialised functions.

Staff work from a range of different bases including their homes, their cars, clients' homes or premises and even sometimes back in the fixed office. Office space is allocated to reflect the tasks and activities which are carried out there, rather than to reflect status or a traditional pattern. It is segmented and specifically designed according to the types of work which are being undertaken.

OTR in its 1996 report, *What new ways of working are made possible by technology?*, found that many organisations which have adopted elements of the virtual office claimed significant gains because of reduced travelling times, fewer distractions and a more creative working environment with more appropriate and effective use of office space.

❑ 2.3 The telecommunications revolution

Today, we have more choice than ever of where, when, how, with whom, and for whom we work. We can communicate almost instantaneously from almost anywhere – by telephone, fax, video or electronic mail – with millions of potential customers and colleagues.

No office today is complete without modern technology. Over the past two decades computers, faxes, printers and scanners have become commonplace. It is estimated that, since 1990, over 12 million computers have been sold in the UK. There are over 2 million fax machines in Britain today. The 1990s have seen rapid development as the computing and communications technologies converge. The potential power of computers increases – microchips are doubling in performance every 18 months – as their costs and bulk decrease.

There has been such rapid technological change in the last few years that in some cases, including the social housing sector, business has not yet caught up with it. Chapter 7 describes in more detail some of the relevant advances, but the most significant include:

- improvements in the range, speed and cost of telecommunications networks;
- the development of the internet for inexpensive global communication and information exchange;
- the development of groupware enabling people, remote from each other but who are part of the same team or organisation, to share information;

- developments of the telephone, producing memory storage, call back features, centralised answerphones and seamless message and call diverts;
- video conferencing which enables people in remote locations to see, as well as hear, each other and so conduct 'live' meetings; and
- computer telephony integration – enabling organisations to 'pull up' customer information from their computerised systems when a customer calls, even before the call centre agent gets involved in answering the call.

The technological aspects are not simple to understand – most staff struggle to grasp the extent of the concepts, let alone understand the potential applications and business benefits on a corporate wide basis. The business environment is the stimulus for change. Technology and new ways of working can enable firms to respond to the new environment, and every organisation in the UK is affected.

The UK Government encourages the use of technologies to generate competitive advantage and itself uses e-mail extensively to communicate between departments and with business partners. The Department of Trade and Industry (DTI) has an extensive internal network linking central and regional offices, which serves around 5000 users. In addition, many government departments such as the DETR are setting up web sites on the world wide web. The DTI is also establishing a video conferencing network linking its central office with regional offices. The plans for the proposed Scottish Assembly aim to make use of the latest technology to improve accountability to, and information for, the public.

The Government's Better Regulation Unit is currently working on a pilot project to develop an interactive electronic form to be used by all departments, as part of its ultimate aim of creating a 'common gateway' for businesses to communicate with any arm of government.

❑ 2.4 Teleworking and telecottages

Teleworking literally means working at a distance. In practice, it means working away from the traditional workplace or office, and communicating with the rest of the organisation using the appropriate hardware and software linked by telecommunications.

When someone is teleworking, they are able to have access to common organisational databases and to share data and work together using groupware. They can communicate through e-mail, video conferencing and telephones, whether they are at home, with customers or at any other location. They can also handle customers' telephone calls which are routed to them by automatic call distribution so that, for example, a tenant calling is unaware that a housing officer is at home, or working at another location, and not in the traditional office.

Teleworking provides the ability to fundamentally re-examine the shape of an organisation. Teleworking, because it involves the redesign of processes, provides significantly enhanced information flows and controls over performance. (Processes are the sequence of activities which organisations undertake in order to meet a specific customer need. They are the specific ways of working – logical groups of activities.)

The next chapter of this Guide explores teleworking and its potential application by RSLs in more detail.

Telecottages, telecentres and satellite offices are alternatives to equipping individual teleworkers to work in their homes. They are centres offering shared multi-media facilities. They may be owned and used by one organisation or run independently and used by a range of employers and workers. Another advantage of telecentres is that they provide some social contact for teleworkers and maintain a work/home divide. These low cost centres are at the heart of the office structure for many organisations – particularly during the transitional phase of changing to teleworking.

❑ 2.5 The flexible office: hot-desking, hotelling and the paperless office

The offices of many social landlords, like those of most organisations, are rarely full. Sickness and holidays may mean that some staff are away; others may be absent at meetings, training courses or conferences; many may be out visiting tenants or inspecting properties. Offices are usually only occupied for eight out of every 24 hours in a day, for two thirds of the days of the year. A survey undertaken by Digital has suggested that 50% of any company's desks were likely to be vacant at any one time and the effective use of office space amounted to just 22%.

Some organisations have tried to solve this problem of under-used space by turning to systems such as **hot-desking**. This means that there are no longer specific desks and offices permanently allocated to individual workers.

Instead, staff who come into the office to work are allocated a workstation for the time that they are working in the office. Hot-desking is a way not only of saving office space and costs, but also of discouraging people from hiding away in offices.

Hotelling, as its name suggests, works on the basis that some employees are often on the road in different parts of the country, yet need periodic traditional office support to hold meetings, plug in their PCs and to undertake desk-based work for short periods of time. Specialist firms in the UK enable the hiring of accommodation as required, even by the hour.

The flexible office addresses the problem of under-use of expensive office space in an even more radical way. The office design reflects what people actually **do** in the office rather than considerations such as status. People do not need to travel to work in order to do work which they could easily undertake at home or elsewhere. They travel to work to meet people or use specific resources. The flexible office, therefore, incorporates several different areas – a reception area, meeting rooms, social facilities and private study rooms. There are no offices or desks allocated exclusively to individuals.

The paperless office is a term used to describe an environment where all communication, document creation and storage is carried out electronically. The paperless office is a reality in many organisations outside the social housing sector. The technology necessary is available, proven, robust and in use in the commercial sectors. The main barriers to its introduction in the social housing sector are: the sector's inability to envisage what the technologies might do for them, resulting in the absence of a sound Information Systems strategy; the lack of technical capability; and the traditional attitudes and resistance of managers and employees.

In the social housing sector, paper is still the main medium for communication. However, this is not the case in some other business sectors which have moved (over the last two years or so) away from paper-based communication. In the social housing sector the time involved in getting letters or memos drafted, typed, sent, considered and answered can be several days. This delay is becoming increasingly unacceptable. Colleagues and customers want to have a much speedier response and there is no technological reason why this should not happen.

CHAPTER 3

TELEWORKING

This chapter describes teleworking in more detail. It examines the different types of teleworking and the posts or functions to which it might be suitable. It also sets out the potential advantages of teleworking from the point of view of the social housing landlord, the teleworkers themselves, tenants and applicants.

❑ 3.1 What is teleworking?

There is no single accepted definition of teleworking. The National Computing Centre defined it as "the use of computing and telecommunications to extend elements of the working environment beyond the traditional workplace" (NCC *Teleworking in the UK* 1992). Some definitions are explicit about the amount of time spent away from the workplace. British Telecom's definition says that teleworking includes spending "a significant proportion of work time away from the employer's premises" (BT *Teleworking Explained* 1993). The Employment Department defines teleworkers as "individuals based at home for at least 50% of their working time" (Employment Department *Teleworking in Britain* 1993).

Teleworking is defined in this Guide as the ability of people to carry out their main duties without having to be based in a traditional office – so that a sizeable part of their working time is spent away from the office. They are only able to carry out their duties by the use of technology such as mobile telephones and networked computers.

Teleworking combines the capability of mobile computers and communications technology to deliver effective and secure solutions for people to work beyond the confines of their offices. Whether from their homes, from tenants' homes, or from local 'telecentres', staff can gain remote access to their corporate computers to send and receive electronic mail or to share information with the rest of the organisation.

❑ 3.2 Where does teleworking originate?

The concept of teleworking was introduced in the UK in the late 1980s, when much of the attention focused on it concerned the business benefits of telework. This differs from the introduction of telework in the United States, where telecommuting was introduced in the early 1970s as a reaction to the oil crisis which the US was then experiencing. Many of the American teleworking initiatives were state ones, where environmental benefits were at least as important as business ones. It is estimated that there are around 11 million teleworkers in the US today (1997 survey by FIND/SVP).

Teleworking is gaining popularity throughout Europe – in Sweden it is estimated that almost 6% of the population are teleworkers (figures from TELDOK, Sweden). In Germany in 1994, it was estimated that 4.9% of the population were teleworkers (EIRR 269, June 1996).

❑ 3.3 How widespread is teleworking?

It is difficult to estimate just how widespread teleworking is. This is partly because different sources define teleworking differently. It is also difficult to get an accurate picture because many surveys exclude part-time teleworkers, or the large volume of 'tacit' teleworking that goes on in organisations which do not have an official teleworking policy. One estimate for this 'hidden' teleworking was that 75-80% of major British employers have 'tacit' teleworkers (Noel Hodson, *Times Magazine*, 12 March 1994).

A Dataquest survey in 1996 suggested that around 50% of companies have some remotely located workers. Other estimates range from 125,000 (OTR, 1996) to 1.3 million (MSF, 1996) teleworkers. Some of these work permanently from home, although experience shows that most successful teleworking mixes working at home or elsewhere with working in the office.

British Telecom forecasts that there will be 3.3 million teleworkers by 2000, with one worker in six using their home as an office, and are currently promoting the ways in which they can assist firms wishing to telework using ISDN (BT research published 1996).

There has been official encouragement for teleworking both nationally and internationally. The Bangemann Report of May 1994 set out specific aims for teleworking in the European Community, seeking 10 million teleworkers by the year 2000 and pilot teleworking centres in 20 cities by the end of 1995, involving at least 20,000 workers. By the end of 1996, however, there was no sign of any significant teleworking centre in any European city. In 1992, OTR forecast that there would be 1.3 million teleworkers in the UK by 1995. In 1996 they reported that there were actually only 125,000.

It is clear that, although it is impossible to find an estimate of the number of teleworkers which everyone accepts, there has been a continuous growth of teleworking. It may be, as one commentator has noted, that teleworking is one of those aspects of information technology that has a slow burning fuse ('Home or Away?', *Computer Weekly*, 23 May 1996).

Example 1: Standard responsive service by teleworking housing officer

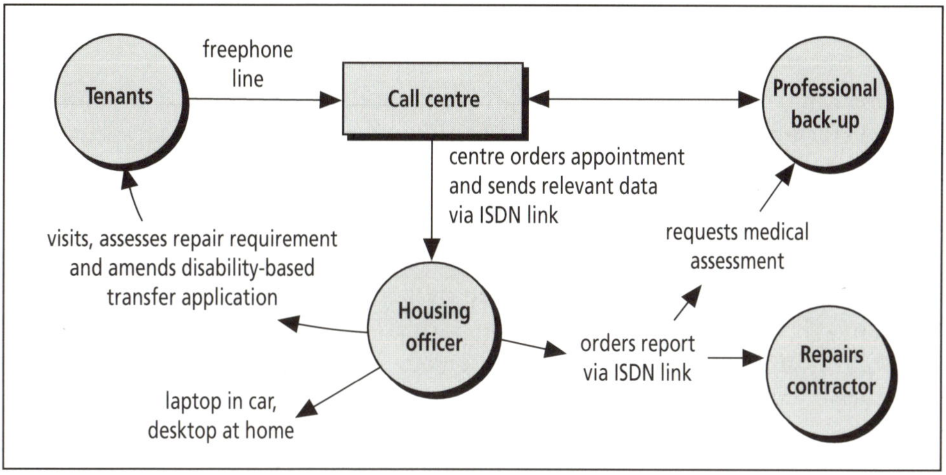

❑ 3.4 A new way of working?

Teleworking means a new way of working for most local authority housing departments and RSLs. Most housing staff work in a head or area office. Staff use this as their base from which they carry out most of the main functions. One effect of this is that many members of the public who want to make use of the services provided by a social housing landlord have to go to the landlord's office rather than have the service come to them, although it is currently estimated that around 80% of the contact which tenants have with their landlord is by telephone.

There are some exceptions to this office-based model. Some staff are often estate based, such as managers and wardens of sheltered accommodation or resident caretakers. These workers cannot be considered as teleworkers, however, as they usually lack the technological support needed to give them instant access to corporate data and to enable them to communicate electronically with colleagues.

The norm for most housing staff is that they start their day by going to their office and this is where they carry out most of their main functions. Many of their main functions are administrative and office based, and could be performed by administrative staff.

Teleworking has the potential to turn this model upside down. It means that working in the head or area office **can** be the exception rather than the rule. It means that more time can be spent working with members of the public providing them with a face-to-face service. It means that more decisions can be made on the spot rather than having to refer questions up the line, providing the worker has the right information, systems and delegated authorities.

All this can be done with the same level of security and reliability as staff would enjoy when working in the office. Teleworking can also help provide a service after office hours.

Teleworking requires a new approach to staff management and monitoring performance. Managers will no longer be able to keep an eye on their staff as they can in most open plan offices. Instead, teleworkers will need to have more delegated power to be able to take decisions. This must be balanced by the introduction of performance measures to control performance.

❑ 3.5 Main types of teleworking

There are four main types of teleworking, all of which could be used by the social housing sector. These are

- working from home;
- working from a telecottage or telecentre;
- working from a distant or remote office; and
- mobile working.

It is worth remembering that the main types of teleworking are not mutually exclusive. A teleworker can both work from home and be mobile.

■ Working from home

Working from home is not unusual. Most managers and other staff work at home from time-to-time, perhaps to complete an urgent report or carry out detailed work which demands peace and quiet which cannot be found in a busy office.

Teleworking from home is not just about taking the odd piece of work home. Instead, it means that much of the person's work, and the equipment they need to carry it out, is based in their own home. The equipment may not be permanently based in the person's home. In fact, more often it is portable, allowing the worker to work in transit too.

It is essential, however, that the teleworker should still have face-to-face contact with colleagues, perhaps through regular weekly trips to the office or working in the office a day or so each week. A 1995 University College Dublin report on teleworking in Ireland found that the most successful teleworkers were those who spent more than half their time working in the office, while teleworkers who operated exclusively from home gave it up because of isolation and poor relationships with management and colleagues. Some of these problems can be reduced by careful planning of teleworking, but the need for some face-to-face interaction between colleagues is a basic one and a teleworking scheme will need to address it.

■ Working from a telecottage or telecentre

As described above, telecottage and telecentres are local centres, often run by an independent agency, which house the technology a teleworker will need to function.

The Telecottage and Telecentre Association (TCA) lists 145 telecottages in the UK, most of which are in small towns serving rural communities. These tend to be used by small businesses or people working from home. The TCA has over 2,000 members and estimates that there are around 10,000 people using telecottages annually.

KC3

KC3, a telecottage in Kington, Herefordshire, processes payroll information for ICI sales teams. It downloads data, processes it and passes it to the BACS clearing system.

A Hackney Telecentre

A telecentre in Hackney in London offers the use of the internet, e-mail and bulletin board services.

Kirklees Metropolitan Council

Kirklees Metropolitan Council set up the Disabled People's Electronic Village Hall in Dewsbury in 1993, to provide training opportunities in IT for disabled people and to provide continued opportunities for them once they were trained for both work and leisure.

The Electronic Village Hall provides a range of services including:

- ten work stations with specialist equipment, software and printers;
- training courses;
- open access;
- demonstrations of software and equipment; and
- advice and help towards employment.

■ Working from a distant or remote office

Here, the teleworker works from a distant or remote office set up by their parent organisation. Rather than equip several teleworkers' homes, the organisation decides to equip one small office which a number of teleworkers can share.

■ Mobile working

The mobile teleworker does not have a fixed base. Instead, she or he works from their car or service vehicle using portable equipment such as a laptop computer and mobile phone. This is ideal for those employees whose jobs require them to build close relationships with customers, such as housing officers, who through mobile working can spend most of their time with tenants rather than travelling or working from the office.

Example 2: Local authority housing service

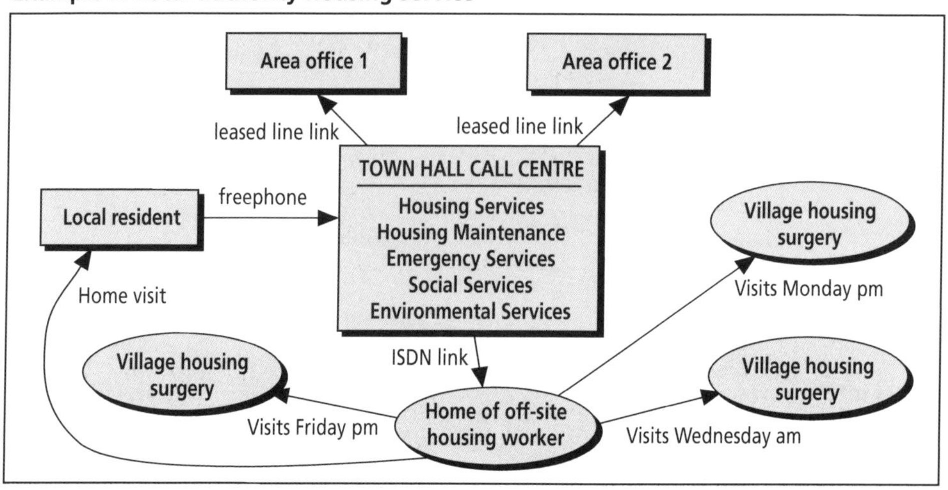

❑ 3.6 Potential teleworking posts

The potential uses of teleworking in the social housing sector are considerable. Examples from other sectors indicate that almost any post could be done by a teleworker. A recent study for the European Commission found that the chief executive of a major British building society now uses his home as his main office, allowing him more time to visit branches and customers. Many repairs operatives now take their laptop and printer with them so they can instantly price work, track down parts and accept payment by credit card. Surveyors usually now operate hand-held computers when inspecting property.

Knowledge Brokers survey of UK-based RSLs and local authorities, conducted in 1997, demonstrated that relatively few social housing landlords had introduced teleworking. Some RSLs had set up remote or distant offices in order to provide a local service in an area which was some way away from an existing area or head office. Most landlords who employ estate-based staff provide them with at least a mobile phone, and sometimes a laptop computer, so they can order repairs or check a transfer request.

The survey also showed that many more social housing landlords were interested in the possibility of introducing teleworking to their organisations. There is no reason why senior managers, allocations staff, surveyors, inspectors, support staff, manual staff and frontline staff (including housing officers and maintenance staff) could not **all** be teleworkers – provided enough care and attention is taken in preparing both the employees and the organisation for the changes teleworking requires.

There is also potential for some staff, who are already working remotely from a social landlord's central office, to benefit from new technology. Wardens of sheltered schemes and hostel workers could have immediate access to information and good communication links with colleagues through laptop computers, modem links or ISDN.

❑ 3.7 Advantages for social housing organisations

Teleworking has a number of potential advantages for local authority housing departments and registered social landlords.

■ Office space

The more a social housing organisation uses teleworking, the less office space it will require. This could produce significantly reduced overheads. Rank Xerox has calculated that for every £1 spent on an office worker's salary, a further £3 goes on overheads.

Teleworking should allow social housing organisations to reduce their demand for office space, but also introduce related working practices which could further reduce costs – particularly more flexible office design.

Of course, organisations will need to provide some office space for their teleworkers. As noted above, most successful teleworking schemes incorporate **some** time spent in the office. Even staff who work predominantly from home, or in transit, will need to work at their organisation's offices from time-to-time and so will require desk space, access to a computer port and so on. Concepts such as 'hot-desking' are one way in which this can be achieved without losing the associated cost savings in office space that teleworking should provide.

■ Devolved structure

Teleworking can help introduce a more devolved structure to social housing organisations. It provides the technology to enable staff to move out of a head office to area-, estate- or scheme-based offices or to enable them to work in transit. At the same time, introducing a more devolved structure can also produce a better service to tenants and applicants by providing a more localised, on-the-spot response to enquiries and problems through instant access to corporate data.

■ Greater customer contact

Teleworking should significantly reduce staff travel time. A recent study showed that the average travel to work distance saved by teleworking is 30 miles per day. (Source: Department of Transport.)

Instead, teleworkers are likely to be located much closer to their customers – tenants and applicants for housing – and so can spend more time dealing with their requests and concerns. This, in turn, should lead to social housing landlords being seen as more human, caring organisations, rather than anonymous bureaucracies where most transactions take place by letter or telephone. Other advantages should include improved debt management, improved information, reduced community instability and the ability to reduce cases of abandonment leaving bad debts and damage to property.

Teleworking also produces environmental benefits. Fewer cars travelling into busy city centres lessens the consumption of fossil fuels, reduces the levels of air pollution and can reduce the numbers of road accidents and injuries. It is estimated that, if nationally 15% of employees teleworked, there would be over half a million fewer car-driving daily commuters travelling in and around London. A 1996 report, *Travel and the Superhighway* (produced for the Autoglass company from information provided by the Henley Centre, British

Telecom and the Institute of Directors), forecasts that car journeys made by commuters and shoppers will drop by 43% by 2010, as more people work and shop from home. Less peak time traffic means that the travel time for essential traffic is reduced too.

■ Increased productivity

Most organisations outside the social housing sector, which have introduced teleworking, claim increases in productivity from 10% to 50%.

There is some evidence to show that teleworking can produce better results. Teleworkers are removed from some of the main distractions which office-based staff face. They will not have to endure the constant ringing of unanswered telephones that is a feature of most open plan offices. They will not be subject to the stream of interruptions which most people can face when they are trying to carry out their main tasks. They will not get caught up in the gossip and intrigue which can flourish in offices.

An Employment Department survey in 1994 found that 47% of managers thought that their teleworkers performed better than their on-site staff, 48% thought that they performed the same, and only 5% thought that they performed at a lower level.

As mentioned earlier, there should be time savings because travelling is reduced. This does not just free largely unproductive time for more productive purposes. Teleworkers are likely to be that much more fresh and alert because they have not spent an hour in their cars or packed in a commuter train. As a result they are likely to provide a better, more effective service.

Evidence also suggests that teleworkers are less likely to take sick leave or time off to care for children or other relatives. Teleworkers mix with fewer colleagues which means the risk of catching a cold, flu or other bug is much reduced. A teleworker may also be able to adjust her or his work pattern round the needs of a sick child or other relative. If the person worked in the landlord's office she or he would probably decide to take the whole day off.

Finally, successful teleworking requires an employer to have a more flexible approach to their employees. Effectiveness is measured by what a person does, not the hours someone spends at a desk or in the office. This enables employees to fulfil commitments they might not normally be able to do. Such flexibility is also likely to mean that the teleworker is more inclined to work in the evenings or at weekends, possibly to attend a tenants' meeting or interview a household seeking rehousing. Moreover, it may enable an employer to retain valued staff. Perhaps a member of staff has become disabled or is undecided whether to return to work after maternity leave. The flexibility which teleworking allows could mean that a social landlord is able to offer the member of staff the opportunity to continue working which traditional, office-based, working might not.

Teleworking should produce additional time available for work. This could enable social housing organisations to spend more time on the longer-term strategic aspects of their work – liaising with likely partners or developing good relationships with contractors for example – rather than only being able to carry out the immediate, urgent, responsive tasks.

■ Maintaining a service

Teleworking has one more advantage which could be useful to some social housing landlords. It allows the organisation to maintain a service during and after a disaster. For example, the landlord's main office may be damaged by fire or flood or may suffer a power cut. If all the staff were office based the organisation would only be able to provide a very limited, emergency service. Teleworking staff, however, would be able to carry on largely as normal. It may even be possible to relocate some head office functions to a teleworker's place of work until the office is repaired.

Example 3: RSL regional director's patch

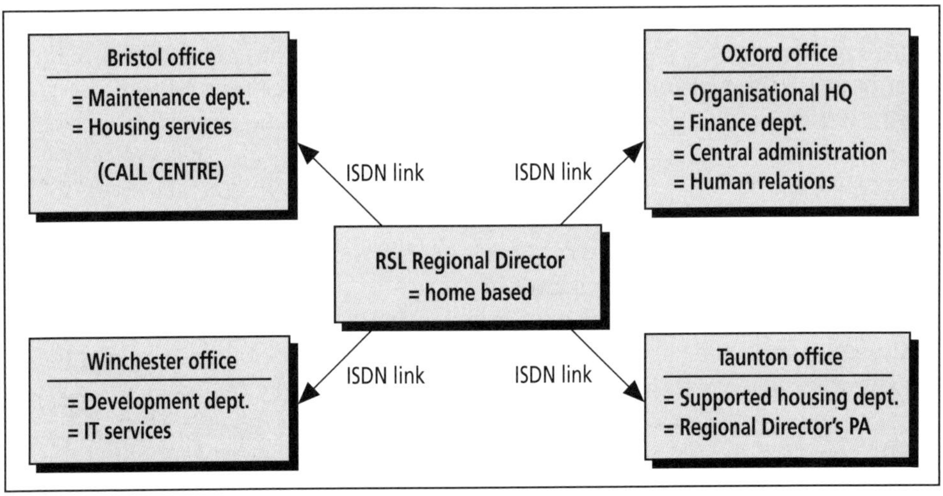

❑ 3.8 Advantages for employees

Teleworking should provide a number of advantages to employees, as well as to their employers.

■ Increased job satisfaction

There is some evidence to suggest that teleworkers gain more satisfaction from their jobs than office-based staff carrying out similar functions.

Teleworkers welcome the flexibility of teleworking, which allows them to get their work done at a time which is, perhaps, more convenient to them than conventional office hours. Flexibility also enables teleworkers to strike a better balance between working and home life.

Teleworkers can also save time by not commuting every day to their offices. This releases an extra hour or two every day, which can be used for more time with the teleworker's family, pursuing leisure activities or carrying out necessary chores. BT suggest that some commuting office workers extend their working year by half – up to 2800 hours – by spending up to four hours a day getting to and from work.

Teleworkers also save money by not commuting everyday. Although some social housing organisations provide staff with a season ticket loan, most employees have to meet their own journey to work travel costs. BT estimates that teleworkers' savings on commuting and clothing can be around £1000 per year.

Job satisfaction is further enhanced by the autonomy of teleworking. Teleworkers are often able to organise their own work far more than office-based staff, who often tend largely to respond to the demands of colleagues and customers. Most teleworkers welcome this. It also helps them manage their time better, and one of the key tenets of good time management is the ability to control how your time is used. A teleworking scheme in one RSL, Sanctuary Housing, takes another approach. Here, administrative staff schedule visits to tenants by mobile housing officers in response to tenants' requests and as part of a planned programme of visits. This frees the housing officers from administrative work, allowing them to concentrate on tenants' needs and use their time better in the field.

■ Less stress

Teleworking can lessen the stress employees face. Several of the main stress factors which employees face spring from working in a conventional office. Being at other people's beck and call, being constantly interrupted, and never being able to find a quiet place to work, are some common causes of stress at work.

Teleworkers are largely removed from these sources of stress. While other stresses may still exist, principally the fear that their computer will crash or their answer machine will develop a fault, these would still be there if the teleworkers were still office based.

There is even some evidence to show that the incidence of repetitive strain injury (RSI) is less among teleworkers. This appears to be because teleworkers are better able to have breaks when they need them and not face the pressure of having to meet deadlines imposed by others.

❑ 3.9 Advantages for tenants and applicants

The main advantage of teleworking to tenants and applicants is that quality of service should improve. Teleworking should mean that staff have more time to devote to meeting tenants face-to-face when that is needed. Of course, many tenant requests can be dealt with very satisfactorily over the telephone, provided that the person answering the call has immediate access to the right information. Responsive and robust information systems, such as call centres which include fast and simple access to the right information through 'screen popping' etc, can deliver this service. Housing officers would then have more time for follow-up visits to tenants about more complex matters such as harassment, nuisance or serious debt problems.

Face-to-face contact is important, not just because tenants and applicants prefer to deal with a person rather than a voice, but because there is evidence to show that customers get a better service when they see someone face-to-face.

Teleworkers should be able to provide a better quality of service because of their ability to call up information or check files on-the-spot. Transfer applicants should be able to find out their points levels and how quickly they are likely to be rehoused. A repairs order can be issued on the spot without having to be routed via a clerk to the contractor.

Tenants could also benefit through reductions in their rent levels – or at least by having smaller rises – from their landlord passing on the long-term savings arising from teleworking.

Currently, most social housing landlords provide a 'skeleton' service out of office hours, possibly using an emergency call system with a duty officer to deal with emergencies. Urgent repairs or reports of harassment are often less promptly handled if they do not occur in office hours. However, tenants may be at work between 9 am and 5 pm or have other commitments that make it difficult for them to make contact with housing staff during office hours. The flexibility that teleworking and the appropriate new technology should bring, enables a social housing landlord to provide an enhanced service at the times tenants need it.

CHAPTER 4

BARRIERS TO TELEWORKING

This chapter looks at some of the main barriers to the successful introduction of new ways of working, including teleworking.

After all, as noted above, teleworking has been heavily promoted both by commercial bodies, such as communications and computer companies, and governments, and yet has failed to grow as rapidly as predicted.

The main barriers to introducing teleworking can be summarised as:

- inadequacies of telecommunications network, hardware and software – and distrust and misuse of technology;
- management attitudes – including managing staff and costs implications;
- staff attitudes – including fears of isolation, damage to career prospects and difficulties in keeping home and work separate; and
- customer attitudes.

❑ 4.1 Inadequate technology

Successful teleworking depends upon having good technological support. In the past, the technical limitations and cost of using the telecommunications network have been a barrier, as has the cost and capability of hardware. There has also been a problem in ensuring firms develop the right software to meet their business needs.

Staff need to access information quickly and know that the information is up to date. The systems in use must be reliable enough to provide service and access around the clock. There must be effective back up and fault-tolerant features in both computer and communications systems, and back up must be available after office hours where the service is critical.

The systems in use must also provide adequate security and have control measures in place against unauthorised access.

Compatible software is essential if teleworkers and office workers are to communicate. Corporate databases must be capable of talking to each other to enable data to flow freely from application to application, thereby providing adequate support to frontline staff.

❑ 4.2 Distrust of technology

Many people working for social housing landlords, including managers, staff and councillors or management committee members, may be sceptical of the benefits of communications technology. Despite the fact that every office has a computer, research undertaken for this Guide showed little appreciation among social housing landlords of how to take advantage of this technology through teleworking. There appear to be two main reasons for this. One is the general failure to utilise the full potential of existing technology. Most social housing landlords do use computers for word processing, housing management databases and maintenance, and rent accounting systems. However, these applications are often not user friendly and do not enable the sharing of data across the various corporate systems, nor the extraction of good management information. The second reason is an inability to understand the capability of technologies in redesigning a business. Social housing providers are very insular and are suspicious of claims made about the use of technology elsewhere. The sector has many examples of unsuccessful IT projects. Some went wrong through poor project management; others because there was inadequate preliminary work in identifying what systems should do. In further examples, organisations seemed to try to introduce systems with significant under investment in program design, project infrastructure, software, hardware and training.

The result is that staff and managers alike are often distrustful of any change in working practices – seeing these as pretexts for shedding jobs – and are particularly suspicious of adopting new technological solutions which promise benefits to staff and customers alike.

This mistrust, and past misuse, of technology are clearly potential barriers to the successful introduction of teleworking.

❑ 4.3 Managing and motivating staff

A report by Incomes Data Services Ltd, *Conservative Management* (1994), concluded that:

> *"Undoubtedly, one of the greatest barriers to the development of teleworking is management resistance. ... Surveys have shown that managers fear a loss of face-to-face contact and difficulties with motivation and discipline. To put it simply, managers have to learn how to trust for teleworking to thrive."* (Teleworking IDS 1994)

Managers may want to be able to use old style techniques of command and control or face-to-face motivation and are afraid that if staff are not 'on-site', they will not be able to do this. In many organisations, a person's work effort is often informally measured, in 'face time' – that is, in how many hours they are seen at their desk.

The successful introduction and implementation of teleworking is likely to require a change in the way staff are managed. It will no longer be possible for a manager to drop by to check that everything is running smoothly. Instead, managers will need to agree targets based primarily on results with their staff. Getting the work done will be more important than being at a desk from 9.00 am to 5.00 pm.

This change could be difficult, both for manager and employee, but it should not be an insuperable barrier. Teleworking will reduce the number of managers in an organisation. Those who remain will be roving coaches and mentors to the teleworkers – helping them to develop both personally and corporately. Teleworkers should receive proper training in the landlord's policies and procedures and have access to concurrent systems which guide the teleworker to get things right first time. Teleworking, if implemented properly, will actually reduce the management overhead of an organisation, as the new practices enable information systems to control workers to a greater extent. Instead of supervisors and managers having to manually compile performance data, processes which have information embedded within them and the information technology tools which can extract performance data, will make data manipulation easier and more automated. This means that organisations can increase the span of control of their managers.

Motivating staff ought not to be a problem either. Teleworking should make it easier for managers to motivate staff rather than the opposite. Some of the advantages of teleworking are increased job satisfaction, more flexibility and less stress – all of which are likely to increase, not decrease, teleworkers' willingness to produce that little bit extra when needed.

■ Staff concerns

Social housing organisations should **not** consider using teleworking for every function. The main application will be for housing management. In addition, some people will not be willing or able to telework.

Some staff may be keen to adopt more flexible ways of working, but others may be reluctant. Attitudes to employment have had to change radically in the last two decades as employees recognise that there is no longer any such thing as a 'job for life'. Most workers have had to develop transferable skills such as computer literacy, teamworking and communication. Nevertheless, adapting to more flexible ways of working, such as teleworking, may be uncomfortable for some people.

Isolation

Employees fear that teleworking will mean they will be isolated from their colleagues, and will not be able to call upon the informal support of colleagues at times of crisis or induction. They feel that not only will they be isolated in this work-related sense, but also excluded from the social interaction associated with any office.

This concern needs to be addressed when planning the introduction of teleworking. Staff working from home or on estates must be able to call upon advice and guidance in the same way office-based staff can. Mobile phones, faxes, e-mail and the internet can all be used to obtain the support a teleworker needs. In addition, coaching and mentoring by managers will ensure that support is given pro-actively. The advent of sophisticated knowledge-based systems, which provide access to the basic core knowledge within an organisation, would be invaluable in supporting housing staff both in the field and in the back office.

The introduction of teleworking does not necessarily mean that individual teleworkers never come into the main office. Indeed, it is important that teleworkers **do** still come into the office at regular intervals. One reason is to maintain some level of social interaction with colleagues. Teleworkers must not be forgotten when it comes to arranging office outings or events. They are still part of the team even if they are not actually based in the same building.

Managers should remember that teleworking does not suit everyone. Some staff do need to be physically part of an office-based team in order to thrive. This should be taken into account when deciding who might telework and who might not. It is also clear that teleworking rarely, if ever, means that **everyone** works out of the office. There will always be a need for a core of office-based staff to carry out key functions.

Damage to career prospects

Some employees believe that teleworking might damage their career prospects, believing that if their managers do not see them every day they will be passed over when promotion opportunities arise or an interesting project needs to be undertaken. This should not happen. Promotion opportunities should be linked to the person's ability to do the job, not whether their manager sees someone every day. Provided teleworkers are managed properly, then there is no reason why they should not be asked to work on a new or interesting project.

Some workers may also be anxious that teleworking is the first step towards 'casualisation', gradually forcing them to become contract or freelance staff. Again, formal documented reassurances should be given to staff before they become teleworkers.

Keeping home and work separate

Employees sometimes worry that teleworking means they will not be able to separate their work from their home life. Tenants and managers may contact them at all times of the day and night. In fact, tenants will not have individual officers' numbers. All calls should be routed through a central number. Managers will need to adopt a disciplined approach to contacting teleworking staff at home – out of hours calls should be restricted to genuine emergencies. Equally, teleworkers must not be allowed to 'hide' from contact with customers and managers. Formal performance protocols may well be required.

Some employers discourage people from becoming teleworkers if they have young children at home, as this could make working difficult. Some teleworkers find that their partners may be hostile to the use of the home as a workplace. Carers may be particularly pressured by attempting to undertake two roles at the same time. Teleworking is clearly not an alternative to securing child care or elder care.

Managing and motivating teleworkers: checklist
❑ Have a clearly defined and communicated vision for the organisation to ensure that **all** staff know the context in which they are carrying out their work and making their decisions – this will particularly help those who are working away from their base.
❑ Articulate clear goals for the organisation to ensure that everyone knows what they have to achieve for their organisation to succeed – this will help staff make those marginal decisions which would often result in them having to unnecessarily consult a supervisor.
❑ Conduct regular and thorough customer perception surveys and disseminate this information to staff so that they know how to improve the service.
❑ Use a structured process of eliciting employees' views and take their views into account when improving the business.
❑ Ensure that all teleworkers spend at least a day or two in the office per week or fortnight.
❑ Have a well designed and deployed appraisal system, which devolves the organisation's objectives to both team and individual levels in the organisation, and which has a good feedback process to ensure objectivity of appraisal – then people know how they are performing and how they need to improve.
❑ Develop managers to become coaches and mentors rather than controllers or supervisors – since homeworkers and in-transit teleworkers will need to feel supported when they are working in the field.
❑ Ensure that only those posts and personnel suitable for teleworking are designated for teleworking – a poor worker will not automatically become a good worker as a result of these new working practices – and address underperformance as part of the performance management processes.
❑ The recruitment and induction processes must be adapted to ensure that not only the right skills, but also the right behaviour, is developed from the outset.
❑ Ensure that the communications and teambuilding processes are adapted to take into account those who are working remotely and that remote workers are included in social events and briefing sessions.
❑ Update the human resources planning process to ensure that the true performance of remote workers and their potential is captured and developed within the overall people development and promotion processes.

❑ 4.4 Governance issues

Local authority councillors and RSL committee members may share some of the reservations about teleworking, or other new ways of working, which managers may have. They may also fear that their own access to staff and information may suffer if staff are not located in the office. One answer may be to extend training and equipment to committee/board members, who will themselves benefit from access to enhanced business information via new technology. For example, instead of merely giving their apologies, committee members could express their views on the agenda reports of meetings that they cannot attend.

❑ 4.5 Setting up and running costs

Another area of concern may be the costs involved. The introduction of teleworking, like the introduction of any change, must be based on cost-benefit analysis. Teleworking requires investment but there is considerable payback within very short periods of time.

The overall investment cost will depend largely on:

- whether the organisation is undertaking a small project or a large project;
- how the project is scoped in terms of providing workers with hardware such as laptops, mobile phones and modem links;
- whether the project looks at network capacity issues, eg, mainframe capacity, dial back etc, access security and response times which will sometimes involve investment in upgrades;
- the extent that the project involves redesigning processes; and
- the extent of the training and mentoring of people to help them adapt to the new working practices.

❑ 4.6 Customer attitudes

Introducing teleworking in social housing organisations will only be successful if it is welcomed by the tenants and leaseholders who are their customers.

As noted earlier, the general public is becoming computer literate and aware that communications and computer technologies enable organisations to move information processing away from the office. In general, if the response to their calls is prompt and effective, most customers do not mind where the person receiving the call is sitting. If social housing landlords' use of technological support enables housing officers to spend less time in the office and more on their patches, most tenants would support this.

If the introduction of teleworking will reduce costs, as indicated by the cost-benefit analysis which the housing organisation has carried out prior to its introduction, this too will be welcomed by tenants and leaseholders.

Case study: Northern Counties Housing Association – Teleworking Pilot

The pilot was implemented in 1998 to measure how effectively a housing officer could provide a mobile service, whilst using their own home as an office base and working to a structured work diary based on local surgeries and regular visits to sites. The mobile housing officer undertook a generic role, covering all aspects of housing management including rent recovery, allocations, void management, tenancy issues, staff supervision and repairs.

Funding for the pilot was supported by the Housing Corporation's Innovation and Good Practice Grant.

The Leeds region of NCHA was chosen due to the large geographical spread of properties across seven local authority areas in west/north Yorkshire and north/north east Lincolnshire.

The pilot patch, Harrogate/Leeds was specifically chosen due to the number of units (433) and type of properties (general needs, family, sheltered) mainly located 17 miles away from the regional office. The Association's Tenants Census indicated a resident need for more personal contact with their housing officer.

To enable objective testing of the pilot, a control patch was also identified at the region's area office based at Scunthorpe. This was similar in size and geographical spread to that managed by the mobile housing officer. As with the pilot patch, performance targets were set and monitored throughout the length of the project.

IT input

The information technology equipment used during the pilot project was as follows:

Hardware

- Pentium laptop PC;
- data cards for local area network, telephone land-line and mobile phone;
- portable desk jet printer;
- static office jet printer;
- digital mobile phone.

Software

- First Housing database. This is the integrated housing management database used across the Association;
- Windows 95;
- Microsoft Office including Schedule Plus. This is used for spreadsheets, word processing and as a networked diary system;
- Microsoft Mail. This is the electronic mail software used across the Association and is isolated to a local area network.

The set up used allowed the housing officer to access live data from the database from any remote location through either a telephone land-line or mobile phone connection. The laptop was linked to the Association's regional file server via the laptop data card dialling into the file server, which is in turn connected to the First Housing database by a kilostream line.

An ISDN link was not used during the pilot so as to allow the project to investigate the feasibility of usage in locations where ISDN is not available. ISDN is now being widely promoted and will be used for any subsequent projects run by the Association whenever possible. An ISDN line is considered to be more appropriate since BT is able to guarantee its stability as a data transfer line. Additionally, there are potential cost savings as an ISDN is charged on data transfer use as opposed to a continually open line.

Operations

- The housing officer was based at home where telephone lines were installed for network links and communications;
- The housing officer worked on a two-week schedule throughout Leeds and Harrogate, this allowed him to attend regular fortnightly surgeries at, or near to, the schemes that he managed;
- Contact was improved with the customer base via the surgeries, but the use of the information technology equipment allowed the housing officer to visit people in their own home and set up a 'mini-office' to access information required during the meeting;
- The pilot project utilised a local rate (0345) phone number, to enable people to contact the housing officer, as an exercise to encourage affordable communication links with the customer base. When the housing officer was away from the home base, calls were diverted to a mobile phone, thereby allowing continued accessibility to the housing officer;
- The nature of the duties of a housing officer require them to visit people in their home, which can expose staff to health and safety risks. The safety of the mobile housing officer was addressed by using a networked diary system, whereby his appointments could be viewed by his line manager and accessed to establish any last known location in the case of any emergencies. The necessity of the mobile phone also provided a vital link;
- The generic role of the housing officer allowed him to deal with the majority of queries, but essentially he remained a distant family member of the regional team and could request the expert assistance of the maintenance team or the welfare benefits advisor if required. The housing officer worked from the regional office one day a week using a hot-desk method to remove the need for a permanent work base.

Essentially, these surgeries allowed the housing officer to take the office to the customer base.

Resident satisfaction

Measure	Pilot "Before"	Target Set	Pilot "After"
Do you know who your housing officer is?	60%	75%	67%
Satisfaction with quality of communication	83%	90%	83%
Surgery useful?	42%	60%	76%
Satisfaction with repairs services	68%	80%	83%

Performance

- For performance, both patches show an improvement in the percentage of voids to rental income. The pilot shows the best improvement with a 20% reduction.
- Over the life of the pilot, the mobile housing officer reduced arrears by 13% (£5402.43). The mobile housing officer has continued to keep voids in line with targets set and reduced voids by seven properties (88%).

Costs

The set up costs for the pilot, including IT equipment and home office items, totalled £4k (including £2265.00 for a laptop).

For office expenditure, both the pilot and control patch performed better than budget. The pilot achieved an underspend of £12,832.00 which can be attributed to savings on salary and computer costs.

Staff consultation/feedback

The mobile housing officer found the workload much harder than anticipated, particularly due to the lettings work involved and quantity of telephone calls received directly on the mobile phone.

If the pilot were to be rolled out, the use of the regional office as a 'call handling service' should be considered, with all calls routed through the office to limit the direct calls. (This would be subject to telephone systems being in place.)

The quality of supervision and delegation of workload were unaffected by the mobile working pattern of the housing officer, primarily due to the weekly team meetings and, secondly, due to the communication systems available. All correspondence is received at the regional office and forwarded in priority order. Microsoft Schedule Plus has been a great monitoring tool for the MHO's planning and activity of workload.

Outcomes

To date, the findings of the pilot have resulted in the following outcomes:

- The mobile housing officer post is permanently established within the Leeds region.

- The concept of remote working utilised for one other officer post, to date, within NCHA.
- Innovations from the pilot have been shared internally among regional offices, e.g. template and network diaries.
- Increased use of laptops for remote working throughout regions.

CHAPTER 5

TELEWORKERS' TERMS AND CONDITIONS OF EMPLOYMENT

This chapter considers, in more detail, the 'people dimension' including trade union views, health and safety concerns, training and security.

❑ 5.1 Trade union views

There has been a mixed reaction from the trade unions to the introduction of new ways of working such as teleworking, with some being generally supportive and others being more cautious. There is a consensus, however, that organisations in both the private and public sectors will increasingly be adopting new, competitive, working practices.

Some unions see teleworking as a means of creating a wide range of job opportunities. The traditional labour market tends to exclude certain people. For instance, single parents find it difficult to work and look after their families. At present, people's needs are generally secondary to the needs of businesses, but teleworking could help to redress the balance.

Case study: Promoting the employment of disabled people

L.B. Enfield introduced the Revenue Homeworkers Scheme in May 1989 to solve problems experienced in recruiting staff to administer the community charge.

They recruited 52 workers who were equipped with a computer, a phone link and office furniture at a cost of £2000 per worker. All workers' homes were visited to check health and safety conditions.

The teleworkers were appointed on the same salary, terms and conditions as office staff, but with an extra one off payment every 18 months. When the posts were advertised, Enfield reported that the number and quality of applicants was higher than for a normal office-based job. Applicants included disabled people, women at home with children and older people.

Two of the first 11 workers appointed were disabled.

Union concern is based on their perception of a long history of the exploitation of home workers by some unscrupulous employers. There is concern that employers will simply use teleworking to reduce costs, including pay and conditions of service, taking advantage of the isolation of individuals to reduce the benefits of being part of a collective workforce. There is also a perceived risk that employers convert employees into self-employed people, thereby shifting more of the business risk on to the teleworker and reducing pay. Clearly, there are good and bad employers and adequate safeguards need to be in place.

Unions have a powerful role to play in supporting teleworkers in respect of issues such as health and safety, insurance, pension and legal advice. Some unions have set up teleworking interest groups with the specific aim of developing services for teleworkers. One union supports its teleworking members with subsidised e-mail and software skills development.

The Manufacturing, Science and Finance Union (MSF) has developed specific guidelines for teleworking, covering such points as the rights of teleworkers to return to conventional office-based working and to enjoy the same terms and conditions as other workers, including access to training.

Unison has also considered the issue in detail, producing a model checklist for negotiating arrangements with employers, which covers matters such as employment rights, health and safety and career development.

The Banking, Insurance and Finance Union (BIFU) have developed negotiators' guidelines, again covering the teleworker's rights and conditions. BIFU's experience of teleworking in the banking sector has fuelled its concerns that changing to telecentres and teleworkers has sometimes involved attempts to undermine existing terms and conditions of employment. Part of a motion to the 1995 Trades Union Congress expressed union concern that "a growing number of employers are imposing 'teleworking' in an attempt to drive down costs at the expense of the workers and evade their responsibilities to provide child care." (See Appendix 2 for details of these documents.)

The TUC advocates home/office combined work for teleworkers because this ensures that teleworkers do not become 'invisible'.

Social housing organisations must ensure that union representatives are kept up-to-date with any change initiative and are involved in its design in order to protect the employment rights of staff.

❑ 5.2 Legal implications

There are a number of legal issues that need to be considered when converting employees to teleworkers.

The first question is likely to be whether teleworkers are still employees or not. The person could be employed either under a contract of employment or as an independent, self-employed, contractor under a contract for services.

A 'rule of thumb' test is that where there is an expectation that continuing work will be provided there is likely to be a contract of employment. If the arrangement is that there is no obligation on either party to provide or accept work, then this is unlikely to be a contract of employment. In most teleworking cases the former is likely to apply.

❑ 5.3 Contracts of employment

Of the RSLs participating in the Knowledge Brokers' 1997 study, only one had a specific contract of employment for teleworkers. Others, even when they employed teleworkers, had not specifically reviewed the contractual position.

Employers are legally required to issue employees with a written statement of employment particulars. This must provide details of the place and hours of work and disciplinary rules which apply to the teleworker. A teleworker's place of work will probably be their home address, which should be specified in the statement. However, the contract needs to provide that the employer may require the teleworker to work elsewhere on reasonable notice. In exercising such a right, it is important that the employer acts reasonably and with sensitivity to the teleworker's circumstances and that incentives are used in appropriate instances.

When implementing teleworking, the social housing organisation and employee may wish to review the employee's hours of work to ensure that they fit well with the organisation's needs. Whilst specifying the hours of employment, the contract needs to take account of one of the objectives of teleworking – which is to increase organisational and personal flexibility. Fluctuating workloads can be addressed, for example, by 'zero hour' or 'annualised hour' contracts. So, for instance, if it is not possible to predict exactly when work will come, then the employer can pay an agreed amount per annum for an overall agreed number of hours over a set time period. The new management processes need to take into account the potential difficulty in monitoring the performance of the contract.

Case study: Leasing company – Lombard North Central

This company carried out a two-year teleworking pilot for a very small number of professional staff. Existing employment contracts were suitably amended and managers visited teleworkers' homes to deal with teleworking and employment issues relating to homeworking. The company achieved a 10% increase in productivity and improved customer satisfaction. In addition, sickness absence declined significantly.

❑ 5.4 Disciplinary procedures

The employer's disciplinary procedures need to be reviewed in the light of the different circumstances of teleworkers. If disciplinary procedures are to be invoked the employer must have the right to insist, at reasonable notice, that the teleworker attends the central office. Internal rules will need to take account of new examples of misconduct that may arise under teleworking, such as the misuse of technology or surreptitiously working for another employer.

❑ 5.5 Monitoring performance

Performance measures, to monitor the output of teleworkers, are important to ensure that they are contributing to the achievement of the organisation's goals to the required extent. This includes using the organisation's resources to the best effect. Misuse of telephones and fax facilities can prove expensive to an employer. Processes need to be in place to minimise abuse by including output monitoring and a right to enter the teleworker's home to assess equipment and the teleworker's activities. Most union guidelines oppose the use of 'spy in the home' mechanisms, such as fitting cameras or key depression monitoring to teleworkers' equipment, to check on the hours worked or other use made of the equipment.

❑ 5.6 Company property

The teleworker must be under a contractual obligation to ensure that the equipment is kept in good condition and that it is properly maintained. The teleworker must be required to return equipment in good working condition upon termination of employment. Organisations should retain the right to recover equipment from the homes of teleworkers. The issue of whether the equipment may be used for personal use is dependent on the policy of the organisation – having taken into account such factors as the increased risk of damage to equipment, the security of data and the employee's taxation position.

❑ 5.7 Restrictive covenants

It is unlikely that a homeworker will require planning permission unless they are constructing an extension to their house for office purposes. However, some homes may be subject to covenants which might restrict their use – but since the public will not be visiting the teleworker's home it is unlikely to cause a disturbance and should not present a problem.

❑ 5.8 Insurance

Most people who are working from home are not covered by their ordinary domestic insurance policies unless they have told their contents insurers that they do work – even to only a small extent – from home. Many insurers are now offering specific home-office insurance policies which will cover equipment, including portable equipment, and business disruption.

❑ 5.9 Equipment

Generally, the employer should provide all equipment. The employer would pay for the costs of setting up the employee at home and also the additional running cost – either directly by paying the bills or giving a fair allowance to employees as part of their contract.

The average cost of equipping each teleworker is approximately £2500. In addition, there are costs of heating, lighting, etc, of approximately £500 to £700 per employee per annum.

Many office and home furniture suppliers have developed ranges of equipment designed for home use at comparatively low cost. Workstations can be purchased for around £300. A separate telephone line is advisable for business use in order to ensure that business calls do not interrupt home life. Where a worker is predominantly mobile, a mobile telephone without the need for an additional domestic line will be sufficient.

❑ 5.10 Pay, tax and national insurance

Most companies, as good employers, pay teleworkers extra to cover the costs of working at home. The general principle should be that the employer fully compensates employees for the additional costs of teleworking. It is advisable to consult the Inspector of Taxes in advance to check the tax and national insurance position of such payments. For example, if equipment provided is not used exclusively for business purposes, it may give rise to a taxable benefit which will need to be accounted for to the Inland Revenue.

New procedures will be needed for teleworkers covering pay, expenses and allowances, sick pay and procedures, holidays and the replacement of company restaurant benefits.

❑ 5.11 Training

The Knowledge Brokers' 1997 survey showed that those RSLs which have introduced teleworking have no specific training strategy for teleworkers and there is no evidence of specific training being provided before implementation.

Employees who are involved in teleworking for the first time usually have a steep learning curve. All teleworkers will need to have some degree of competence in respect of information systems and a sound knowledge of the corporate software and telecommunications upon which they are dependent. It will be essential to match the time and money allocated to the development of teleworkers, to those skills which will have the greatest impact on the performance of the individual. Although there is generally increasing emphasis on employees taking responsibility for their own skills development throughout their careers, employees will still largely depend on employers to provide the training that they need and to pay for it.

However, the specialist nature of teleworking means that few organisations implementing teleworking for the first time will have the ability to deliver internal training to the appropriate standard. Employees may, therefore, learn most from outside specialists in this area. It will also be necessary to re-skill the training department, personnel and other key managers.

Case study: Computer hardware supplier – Digital Equipment Corporation (DEC)

This company says it has saved £16m and increased its productivity by around 30% as a result of teleworking. The UK operation has one third of its staff teleworking, of which just under 50% are homeworkers. It provides two courses specifically for the teleworker: one to help them make the transition from office working to homeworking and the other covers the use of technology and new processes.

Case study: Housing 21

Housing 21 primarily deals with housing for elderly people by way of sheltered schemes. Each scheme is managed by either one or two resident managers. Most schemes either have a small office on site or the resident managers work from their own homes within the schemes. However, at present they cannot be considered teleworkers because they do not have access to appropriate communications technology.

Housing 21 has six field-based housing services managers working from sheltered housing schemes who are provided with mobile phones, faxes and a PC linked to the housing management, rents and other systems.

Data held on the field workers' PCs includes housing management, rents and service charge information directly relating to the region in which the field worker is operating. This information is updated overnight.

Staff are selected according to normal criteria but, in addition, applicants must be considered to be able to work in isolation from other colleagues for most of the week.

Housing 21 believes that managers of teleworkers need to be good at objective setting, monitoring performance and establishing good reporting mechanisms. They also need to be available for advice and good at motivating staff.

Support systems for teleworkers provide for their inclusion in meetings based on a requirement that they attend regional offices one day a week for familiarisation, training and discussion; and full involvement in social events.

Current drawbacks include the occasional delay in giving and obtaining information. Also field workers suffer from not having access to an e-mail facility. Housing 21 attempts to overcome these issues through enhanced people-processes rather than additional technology. There is a designated regional-office-based colleague responsible for ensuring the communication flow is efficient. The absence of e-mail is currently limiting the use made of data.

Housing 21 notices that field staff feel more motivated and more confident when they have the same information as 'back office' customer service staff.

Training teleworkers, managers and other staff
• Ensure that the induction process for new staff includes sound briefing on how the organisation links together and provide named points of contact – put this information on the organisation's intranet wherever possible.
• Never place new staff in the field working on their own – ensure that they spend the early stages of their career working either in the more traditional office environment or working alongside an experienced colleague in the field, until they are familiar with working practices.
• Train remote workers well in the use of the supporting technology and, most importantly, ensure that they know how to fix simple problems with technology when they are in the field.
• Ensure they are trained to use the software and hardware to its full capabilities.
• Ensure that remote workers are soundly briefed in the organisation's policies and processes so that they have the minimum dependence on 'helpdesk' support infrastructure and people back at base.
• Ensure that teleworkers are allocated a mentor to help them develop their skills and to give them someone with whom they can talk through any issues or problems.

❑ 5.12 Health and safety

Given the remoteness of teleworkers, new management processes will be required to provide for the increased care of teleworkers, ensuring that there is frequent contact and communication with teleworkers and that the employer is receptive to any health and safety issues which arise. There must be equal ease of access to human resource counsellors and personnel staff as there is in the traditional office.

Health and safety legislation requires the employer to ensure that there are adequate safeguards in place to protect the health and safety of employees. All places of work should have an approved safety statement. The employer must inspect all equipment regularly to ensure that it is safe. In respect of teleworking the employer's obligations can be met through a contractual right of entry to the place of work, health and safety questionnaires and training courses. The employer may also safeguard their position by supplying all working furniture, thereby ensuring that it complies with all relevant regulations.

Teleworkers will themselves be anxious to keep their home/workplace safe and will respond positively to guidance and advice. A risk for everyone using technology is repetitive strain injury (RSI). Employers must support the teleworker in setting up their workstation and ensuring that it complies with all appropriate regulations. Continuous monitoring is also essential. Relevant regulations and guidance such as the Health and Safety (Display Screen Equipment) Regulations 1192 which implement a European Directive, are applicable to teleworkers as well as office-based staff, if they are required by their employer to use a workstation at home.

Where the mobile worker is required to use a mobile telephone when travelling in their car, the employer should ensure that there is a hands free facility to avoid breach of motoring laws.

Employers should establish a process to enable teleworkers to report accidents or hazards in a similar way to office-based staff. Hazards such as trailing cables must be identified and eliminated. Only 50% of registered social landlords surveyed had rules in place concerning the work environment of staff that were home-based.

❑ 5.13 Security

It is sometimes assumed that any computer which is not based in an organisation's office, but which can access information stored there, automatically jeopardises security and confidentiality. There is no reason why this should be the case.

Teleworking does not present a new security risk. After all, in most organisations, people can walk out with diskettes, laptops, files and anything else in their briefcases or bags. The selection of teleworkers and their training can ensure people take responsibility for keeping information confidential and secure. It may also be a good idea to provide teleworkers with lockable fireproof filing cabinets or disk boxes. Where the teleworker is mobile, they are likely to take their laptop into a tenant's home with their mobile telephone so that they can access appropriate forms and data. However, on the rare occasions where they do not do so, for security reasons the equipment should be locked in the boot of the car.

Potential breaches of security can be minimised using solutions such as passwords, access codes and careful monitoring. At the same time social housing organisations have to recognise that no system is foolproof and determined hackers can tap into even the most advanced office-based systems.

CHAPTER 6

IMPLEMENTING CHANGE

This chapter looks at the steps which social housing organisations should take if they are considering introducing teleworking and associated changes in ways of working, looking in particular at:

- implementing teleworking for some posts;
- implementing some system of hot-desking or flexible office design; and
- encouraging moves towards a 'paperless' office.

❑ 6.1 Introducing new ways of working

Introducing new ways of working, such as teleworking, is no different from other change programmes in that the organisation: should undertake a formal business justification process, including carrying out a cost-benefit analysis and a feasibility study; should plan its deployment needs effectively and decide how performance will be measured and benefits will be monitored. It is important to remember that whilst new ways of working can make a good company better, inappropriate and badly implemented changes could make a poorly managed organisation worse.

Knowledge Brokers research suggests that RSLs are not conducting rigorous cost-benefit analyses before deciding whether or not to proceed with individual change strategies. Some 20% of the RSLs surveyed for this Guide said that they are planning to implement teleworking in the near future, but none have yet compiled a formal business case. These organisations will either implement teleworking as part of an organisational structure review to improve service delivery **or** as part of a customer service improvement project to establish a call centre.

In some cases, the change initiatives highlighted by the research were inconsistent with other strategic imperatives. For example, most RSLs have strategies to increase customer contact and to reduce overall operating costs. However, quite reasonably, many customer care policies included lengthening office hours, provision of dedicated freephones and improved home visiting arrangements. These policies were not always consistent with the strategy of cutting costs. However, introducing teleworking could improve customer contact **and** reduce costs.

Case study: North British Housing Association

North British Housing Association, whose head office is based in Preston, has recently carried out a review of its information system requirements. As a result, a project has been set up to replace its existing information systems, with a new fully integrated housing and financial management system designed to support all of its key functions. The Association will also be expanding its use of local area networks across the country – providing a basis for increasing its use of office systems to share information. This investment is designed to support the organisation in achieving its key objective of providing an improved service to customers and to exploit the benefits of new technologies for organisational administration. As part of this wider programme of exploiting new technology, the Association has also been experimenting with the use of video conferencing to reduce the need for senior staff to travel long distance for meetings.

Case study: English Churches Housing Group

The English Churches Housing Group (ECHG) business strategy focuses on the tenants' needs and aspirations and in making contact easier and more effective.

ECHG has decided that teleworking is integral to the achievement of these goals and intends to commence the implementation process within the next six months. ECHG considers that the main benefits from teleworking are improved customer service through increased productivity and reduced operating costs, particularly office costs. ECHG has carried out a cost-benefit study to determine the case for teleworking and expects to recover its investment within two years.

ECHG is planning to give laptops to teleworkers and considers that e-mail and electronic workflow are essential to the sound functioning of teleworking. It also considers that improved information flows will lead to improved customer service.

ECHG believes that teleworking is most appropriate for social housing in the areas of housing management and housing maintenance.

Currently all data is held on a mainframe computer, but the organisation's move to client server technology will place it ideally for teleworking.

ECHG considers that sound performance indicators are essential. It acknowledges that there may be some disadvantages associated with the change in management style, the need for dedicated office space in the home and the potential for social isolation.

❑ 6.2 Making the case for change

The following questions need to be addressed when considering changing working practices.

Should we consider teleworking and other new work practices for our business?
Yes. An initial analysis is worthwhile even if only to confirm that new practices are not appropriate at present. Housing organisations will want to assess whether the various options are relevant to their own organisation and what pressures for change are likely to emanate from their operating environment.

What are the main reasons for changing the way we work?
There must be a business imperative driving change, together with leadership and determination at board or committee level. The final result should be enhanced performance through improved tenant services and closer customer contact, while reducing and then maintaining lower operating costs, including potential reductions in fixed overheads.

For example, RSLs, including the smaller ones, which may be expanding rapidly are able to grow with less capital investment in buildings and associated infrastructure.

Other reasons might include improved lifestyles for employees, with more control over their work and more flexibility; environmental considerations including less pollution, better use of office space and less traffic congestion; and finally improvements in the price, capability and robustness of technology.

What if we decide not to make any changes?
It is still essential to monitor the organisational culture of business competitors and to identify key external events that will trigger a reassessment, such as the price and capability of technology.

Pros and cons of teleworking	
Pros	**Cons**
Teleworking creates an organisation which is much more responsive to customer needs and flexible to varying demands.	Teleworking, without soundly designed information systems and the right technology and training, can lead to a significant breakdown in communications between the centre and individual workers.
Properly implemented with the right information systems, teleworking can enable employees to be more productive and provide a high quality service.	Teleworking necessitates the redesign of key parts of the organisation's processes, organisation structure and job roles.
Teleworking frees office space either for sale or for new activities, thereby generating significant cost savings for the organisation.	The organisation's key strategies, in particular the human resources and information systems strategies, need to be revisited to accommodate the newer technologies and working practices that enable teleworking.
Teleworkers spend much less time on back office administration and much more time face-to-face caring for tenants and applicants.	A sound technology maintenance programme, which focuses on a highly flexible and responsive service that is field-based, is essential.
Teleworkers, if they are trained properly in their work and selected according to the right psychological characteristics, usually derive much greater job satisfaction than traditional office workers.	Social inclusion in occasional social events and team meetings is essential to maintain a sense of belonging and organisational cohesion. →

Pros	**Cons**
Teleworkers, given the right equipment and training, may be significantly more productive than traditional workers.	Without well planned and executed implementation of teleworking there is (at worst) a risk of breakdowns in tenant service and (at best) a failure to realise the benefits to be derived from teleworking.
Teleworkers can have better home lives because they spend less unproductive time travelling.	Communications processes involving employees should be redesigned to avoid those working at the centre having information which those in the field do not.
Better relationships with tenants are generated through teleworking and estate problems are identified and tackled more quickly.	Investment in the right telecommunications technologies is essential.
Because teleworkers have well developed technology and customer management skills they are marketable and can have better career prospects.	Whilst piloting teleworking identifies areas which can be addressed before full implementation, too much of a 'toe in the water' approach may lead to lip-service rather than real business benefits.
Managers can re-focus on coaching and facilitating employees to a greater extent rather than traditional, costly management approaches such as being information providers and controllers.	A well structured and information-based external communications programme involving all stakeholders, including council or committee members, is essential to avoid a perception that things are happening in secret.
The teleworking organisation usually cuts its cost structure and focuses on value adding activities.	Organisations often mistakenly assume that teleworking is focused solely on working at home. However, in many instances the greatest benefits from teleworking are from mobile working – that is working whilst in transit or on customers' premises.
Collaborative working technologies, necessary to support teleworking, can significantly increase organisational learning and innovation.	
Teleworking has environmental benefits.	

❑ 6.3 What makes a successful teleworking scheme?

There is more to successful teleworking than merely giving a member of staff a laptop computer and a mobile phone.

The Department of Employment carried out a survey to determine the preconditions for successful teleworking schemes. The elements which they identified were:

- a relationship of trust between manager and teleworker;
- clearly defined goals and expectations;
- regular and well-established communication patterns;
- regular face-to-face meetings, both with managers and other team meetings;
- close integration into the corporate culture, including participation in appraisal schemes and training programmes;
- work which carries some intrinsic job satisfaction; and
- good personal reasons for the teleworker to spend some time at home.

Only if a housing organisation is reasonably confident that it can build these factors into the design of the teleworking programme, should they embark upon teleworking.

❑ 6.4 Key steps for introducing teleworking

Checklist for introducing teleworking

- ❑ Inform workforce, board or management committee and customers about programme.
- ❑ Carry out a feasibility study and cost-benefit analysis.
- ❑ Decide which posts are suitable for teleworking and whether to introduce teleworking throughout the entire organisation or only in some departments/areas.
- ❑ Carry out a pilot study.
- ❑ Evaluate the pilot study and amend implementation plan in the light of the pilot.

→

- ❑ Communicate results of pilot to workforce, management committee and customers.
- ❑ Select teleworkers.
- ❑ Equip teleworkers by providing training as well as communication support, suitable equipment and an appropriate working environment.
- ❑ Ensure contracts and other terms and conditions reflect new business circumstances.
- ❑ Review provision of office facilities for teleworkers when needed.
- ❑ Set up effective mentoring, coaching and support systems.

■ Inform workforce, board or management committee and customers about programme

There should be communication and consultation with staff, board or committee members and customers throughout the process of introducing teleworking. This will help to counter rumours and encourage a more positive attitude to the planned changes. Staff and customers may have pertinent observations about service delivery which impact on the proposals for teleworking. In addition, feedback from as wide an audience as possible is essential to evaluate the success of the pilot and to identify any problems as teleworking progresses. Communication could be through briefings, newsletters or training sessions.

The whole programme needs to take into account the likely response of employees to the implementation of teleworking. Employee unions should also be consulted and involved in the implementation as far as possible. Consultation should stress that teleworking **is not** a staff 'perk' or an entitlement. It **is** a different way of working.

Consultation carried out both before and after the pilot, and during and after implementation of teleworking, should address the concerns which staff may have, such as those discussed in Chapter 4. Staff should be involved in the design of the programme and the implementation process – supported by appropriate specialist resources from within and external to the organisation.

■ Carry out feasibility study and cost-benefit analysis

The feasibility study should provide an outline implementation plan covering the main stages such as:

- identifying the processes and jobs potentially suitable for teleworking;
- selecting the appropriate technology;
- whether or not there should be a pilot project;
- determining how the project will be resourced and organised;
- anticipating the timescales in which the benefits will be realised;
- implementing the staff selection process, training and contractual changes;
- procuring and installing equipment; and
- implementing support for teleworkers, including equipment maintenance.

Case study: A UK water company – cost-benefit analysis

This company has the need to deliver core products and services, of the appropriate quality, to customers at a time when there is increasing demand for improved customer service and a need to reduce operating costs and the cost of customer care.

The vision for teleworking was to enable all the field forces to work from their vehicles and from their homes, communicating via the mobile phone network and e-mail.

Frontline employees are now empowered by having the right information at the right time and, therefore, are able to deal much more effectively and faster with customer needs.

Knowledge-sharing across the business chain takes place and the availability of more customer information contributes substantially to increased productivity and improved customer service. There is also a reduction in the need to travel to depots.

The field force has enhanced technical information which they access over their mobile phones linking them into the corporate database – including access to digitised maps of where pipes are, so they can locate them quickly and then fix them – to assist them in making more decisions.

Data is captured at the point of job execution and is validated. The data includes information on what the nature of the repair was and when it was fixed, which is then communicated via mobile phone to the central database. The data is then made available to the call centre, etc, so that its staff can answer customer queries.

Improvements in data integrity (accuracy of data) have been achieved because the fieldworker inputs the information and thereby eliminates the need to enter the data from hand-written sheets etc, which will result in time delays and errors in recapturing data.

The field force also benefits from enhanced safety, especially where working alone. The exact status of each person is known and automatic alarms can be raised where visits to customers fall outside predefined parameters. This capability also extends to the contractors as part of the virtual workforce.

The norm has become that office workers will work from home, wherever feasible, and they have to justify the right to office space. Significantly fewer premises and depots are required. Non-strategic premises are being sold wherever possible.

This is the summary of the cost-benefit case for the teleworking programme of the organisation described in the case study above.

Business area	**Number of field force**	**Payback over 5 years Discounted at 10% £**
Network and waste inspectors	200	5 million
Customer service representatives	50	1 million
Mains and services	250	3 million
Credit management	50	1.5 million
Water sampling	30	no benefit
Sludge management	30	no benefit

Network and Waste* Inspectors Calculation of Cost-Benefit							
Costs & benefits	**Year 0**	**Year 1**	**Year 2**	**Year 3**	**Year 4**	**Year 5**	**Total**
Costs	**£**	**£**	**£**	**£**	**£**	**£**	**£**
Hardware	862k						862k
Installation	20k						20k
Software	300k						300k
Training	127k						127k
Redeployment	122k						122k
Annual charges	177k	177k	177k	177k	177k	177k	1.062m
Total Costs	1.608m	177k	177k	177k	177k	177k	2.493m
Benefits							
Productivity	637k	1.273m	1.361m	1.450m	1.450m	1.450m	7.621m
Transport charges	90k	180k	180k	180k	180k	180k	990k
Data integrity	59k	118k	118k	118k	118k	118k	649k
Avoided IT charges			70k	10k	10k	10k	100k
Total Benefits	786k	1.571m	1.729m	1.758m	1.758m	1.758m	9.360m
Net Cash Flow	(822k)	1.394m	1.552m	1.581m	1.581m	1.581m	6.867m
Cumulative Cash Flow	(822k)	572k	2.124m	3.705m	5.286m	6.867m	
Discounted Cash Flow @ 10%	(822k)	1.268m	1.288m	1.186m	1.075m	980k	4.975m
Cumulative Discounted Cash Flow	(822k)	446k	1.734m	2.920m	3.995m	4.975m	

* Mobile working

■ Decide which posts and departments are suitable for teleworking

A housing organisation might begin by examining those areas of its business which demonstrate the greatest potential for performance improvement and where improvement would contribute most to the overall achievement of the organisation's strategy and key performance measures. It is usually within the housing management and maintenance areas that the social housing organisation will benefit most from adopting teleworking.

Having determined the areas where there would be the greatest impact, the organisation should then identify whether the process (when redesigned) would be suitable for teleworking. Areas should be those where outputs can be easily measured, where electronic communication is feasible and where daily face-to-face interaction with colleagues is less important. Possible posts might be allocations staff, repairs and maintenance clerks and inspectors, estate officers and tenant participation staff.

The organisation might also decide to introduce teleworking on a phased basis – either to different geographical areas or to different functions. It is, however, important when taking a phased approach to ensure that each phase is allowed a sufficient, but not overgenerous, timescale to ensure that tangible performance improvements are achieved.

■ Carry out a pilot study

Piloting a teleworking project provides the opportunity to resolve likely problems before full implementation. However, it is important that the goals and timescales are sufficiently challenging to ensure that the pilot is not just a token trial. The length of time set aside for the pilot stage depends upon the ease with which the results can be measured. Management needs time to adapt from face-to-face management to results management. The length of the pilot also depends on how different the new ways of working are, compared with the existing ways and how new the technologies being adopted are to the organisation.

Piloting allows the risks of teleworking to be identified and appropriate measures to be taken to manage these risks. Teleworking pilots usually involve experienced employees rather than new staff, because they know how the organisation works and because they are a known quantity to the organisation. Although staff should be volunteers, it is important to ensure that they will give unbiased feedback if the organisation is to learn anything significant from the pilot.

An experienced project manager with clear responsibilities should be appointed to run the pilot, together with reporting arrangements to a sponsoring senior manager. Specialist consultancy support may be needed in some or all stages of the project, particularly at the outset. It is important that the project is soundly resourced and that all project members have clear role definitions and responsibilities. It is imperative to use a structured project methodology, which will go a long way in removing risks and ensuring value for money is achieved.

Before the pilot starts, it is essential to define the measurable success criteria against which it should be judged. Experience shows that organisations which hurry the planning and implementation of a pilot, are often unable to make an objective assessment of its results and, indeed, often fail to achieve business benefit.

Staff, who are unlikely to be directly involved in teleworking, also need to be informed of the reasons for introducing teleworking, who the project manager is, the anticipated outcomes and how performance will be measured.

■ Evaluate the pilot study

The pilot must be properly evaluated to see what changes should be made to processes, technology and management support or if full implementation of teleworking should go ahead at all.

Case study: Britannia Building Society

In April 1995, Britannia initiated a pilot scheme to examine the feasibility and costs of working at home for audio typists. Documents, dictated during the day by central office staff, are automatically down loaded each night to the PCs of home-based audio typists, and the transcripts returned by modem for printing.

The pilot involved 12 volunteers from three departments and was so successful that Britannia is planning to widen its use of teleworking.

■ Select teleworkers

Most organisations which have a policy and procedure for teleworking, use selection criteria to decide whether an employee can work away from the office. Selection criteria usually cover:

- suitability of the job – can the job be done away from the office with remote supervision and with results that can be observed or measured in some way?
- personal qualities and characteristics of the employee – can the person motivate themselves to work with little supervision? Are they happy to take on responsibility? Employees must also have worked for the organisation for some time; been part of the same team/department for some time; be self-motivated and happy to work away from the physical office environment; and be happy to integrate home and work life and find it easy to stop and start work;
- suitability of the home for teleworking – the size, possible distractions and safety of the work area; and
- cost implications – introducing teleworking for a post should not increase its costs, taking all possible savings into account.

Some organisations use psychometric testing to assess whether individuals are suited to teleworking. In general, good workers make good teleworkers. If someone is performing badly in the office, it is unlikely they will function well away from the office. All teleworkers must be volunteers, but wanting to telework does not mean that someone is capable of teleworking. All staff must be assessed.

■ Equip teleworkers by providing training as well as communication support

People must have the right equipment to do the job and the skills to use the equipment. Staff may need training and retraining to use the hardware and software – it will not be as easy to ask for assistance as it is in the office, although they should have on-line help to enable them to use their systems effectively.

Case study: Riverside Housing Association

Riverside Housing Association has, in recent years, recognised the need to improve the quality of service provided to its tenants whilst controlling and, where possible, reducing costs.

Riverside considers that its ability to remain competitive, whilst providing excellent standards of service, will largely depend on the successful use of new technology.

Riverside undertook a year-long pilot project in 1995/96 which incorporated innovative use of new technology, including a freephone facility for tenants, a modem link to a maintenance contractor and the facility to dial in to the housing management core system from local 'surgeries', which were held to accommodate tenants who required direct access to staff and services. A comprehensive housing management service was provided for around 1000 units of property.

Following the pilot project, Riverside decided to investigate the viability of introducing a telephone-based customer services centre (CSC), which would provide a first point of contact for the majority of enquiries from tenants. This service would be provided 24 hours a day, 365 days a year.

Preparatory work has encompassed process analysis and redesign, specification of telephony requirements, including computerised telephone integration (CTI), and automatic call distribution. Voice mail has also been introduced to the Association. Research conducted included statistical information on customer satisfaction levels, analysis of existing telephony patterns as well as analysis of the financial, human resource and cultural implications of this proposed major change in working practice.

Riverside has concentrated its IT resources on the introduction of the CSC rather than teleworking. However, many of the technical innovations which have been mooted are in themselves likely to encourage the trend towards teleworking, particularly the introduction of e-mail, groupware, voice mail and laptop computers.

The benefits of the new call centre will only meaningfully be evaluated after the pilot has run for a reasonable period. A structured evaluation process will be undertaken using the data collected during the initial months of the project as a benchmark.

■ Ensure contracts and other terms and conditions reflect new business circumstances

Once agreement to the changes has been reached, the contractual arrangements need to be dealt with. This can range from issuing a completely new contract to simply drafting a variation to the existing contract. Responsibilities for the cost of the new technologies and the upgrade of the telecommunications infrastructure need to be determined.

Some organisations draw up a code of practice for teleworking covering employee obligations, management obligations, trade union representation, contact with the office, health and safety, security, career development, pay and conditions. The code could also cover practical details such as accommodation, planning regulations, tax implications, insurance, and equipment.

■ Review provision of office facilities for teleworkers when needed

This may involve the introduction of flexible office design or hot-desking – see below. The space available for teleworkers, when they are in the office should both be sufficient for their needs and welcoming. Teleworkers will need access to equipment in the office such as the photocopier and fax machine, as well as office supplies and refreshments.

■ Set up effective mentoring, coaching and support systems

It is important that teleworkers continue to feel part of the organisation. They should receive the same information as office-based staff and at the same time. Training, social events and general news should go promptly to all teleworkers. Teleworkers should be invited to be members of working groups or committees in the same way that office-based staff are. Support systems should ensure that there is regular, informal contact with managers, coaches and mentors, as well as more structured review sessions. Teleworkers should be part of any appraisal and personal or career development systems which are in place.

Experience suggests that managers often only give feedback on a teleworker's performance when there is an issue to be resolved, and in some instances teleworkers can be left out of the celebration of organisational successes, such as when a new contract is won. Teleworkers need to be part of a teambuilding process and communications are vital for this. Personalised numbers, that automatically route calls to wherever the worker is based at a point in time, will avoid the need to publish people's personal numbers yet still keep them in touch.

Conversely, colleagues of teleworkers may need to be kept in touch with what the teleworkers are producing, so that they do not become resentful of those teleworking. Teleworkers should be encouraged to use the phone, e-mail and visits to stay in touch with their colleagues.

One of the most common difficulties when introducing teleworking is concern from middle managers, who may feel that their status is threatened with the extent of employee empowerment and the loss of staff visibility and increased emphasis on results.

Retraining for both management and staff will be required to enable them to adapt successfully to teleworking. Considerable focus should be placed on effective communication. Enhanced managerial skills in delegation, co-ordination and the management of results will be needed. Specific management training may need to cover objective setting, performance related pay and improved interpersonal skills.

Where, for example, part of a department or team teleworks, it is critical to build a single departmental team to avoid the development of divisive behaviour or a 'them' and 'us' feeling between office-based staff and teleworkers. Managers need to be sufficiently close to teleworkers to understand when there is a problem. A sound teleworking process should include many face-to-face meetings.

There should be on-going management contact with teleworkers to deal with:

- agreeing objectives and performance improvements;
- performance reviews;
- establishing pay and bonuses; and
- staff counselling and training.

Case study: A major bank – Lloyds TSB

This bank started a pilot teleworking scheme in 1992. This involved a small number of volunteers from their Information Systems Department. Now about 50% of the total department's workforce are teleworking for an average of two to three days a week.

The bank created a multi-disciplinary team of employees across the organisation to address issues such as health and safety, personnel and telecommunications.

Case study: Information systems company – Siemens Stockholm

This company decided to move to a new location. After consultation with the trade unions, a teleworking programme was introduced over the following year.

One third of the staff now telework including the managing director. Applications to telework had to be submitted, in the first instance, to the relevant line manager whose decision was subsequently confirmed by the managing director. Teleworkers are required to spend at least one day a week at the office. The costs of equipment and the associated charges are met by the company but any other costs are met by the employees.

Case study: Metropolitan Housing Trust

Metropolitan Housing Trust introduced teleworking in 1994/95 and is one of the largest social housing organisations to implement teleworking. Staff teleworking within Metropolitan include managers and directors working from home, staff in care homes, support housing, housing management, estate regeneration, repairs and maintenance and project staff. The Trust is now adding a number of small satellite offices as part of estate regeneration projects.

Teleworkers are provided with e-mail and access to their central databases, although they cannot currently download corporate data on to their PCs. Security precautions for teleworkers include dial back facilities and passwords on networks and applications. The Trust is satisfied that data integrity is at least as good as when everyone worked in an office. Metropolitan has just been through a period of major IT investment and expects to see the payback in two to three years.

Metropolitan has adopted teleworking for reasons of cost saving and tenant service improvement, particularly since it allows the Trust to provide a local service when otherwise it would not be able to. The Trust has reduced overheads, including travel costs and secured closer and more regular customer contact. Information on tenant arrears has become more current and rent collection more effective.

❑ 6.5 Introducing hot-desking

Some organisations have introduced hot-desking to gain the opportunity of making savings on the use of space. These savings can then be utilised to improve the equipment and facilities in the office. The main barrier to the successful introduction of hot-desking is that some staff have strong territorial instincts and feel uncomfortable or threatened without personal territory. Experience suggests that this barrier can be removed by a planned introduction of hot-desking, by having a 'desk sharing' approach where two staff share one desk, and by ensuring that there is some 'club' style accommodation available where people can meet, have refreshments and take part in the social side of work.

Checklist for introducing hot-desking or other flexible office designs

- ❑ Look at how the office is currently used and consider different approaches.
- ❑ Consult staff.
- ❑ Reduce the number of desks and individual offices to the number consistent with the maximum amount of people working in the office at any one time.
- ❑ Meet need for 'quiet space' – group meeting, training, drop-in areas and equipment.
- ❑ Operate a booking system for access to desks – via e-mail, fax, telephone or an office manager.
- ❑ Ensure all mobile staff have portable communications equipment – especially phone systems that can connect with particular staff wherever they sit.
- ❑ Provide secure storage space for personal property and work equipment.
- ❑ Monitor what is happening and make adjustments to, for example, the booking system.

■ Look at how the office is currently used

This task requires the housing organisation to look at how it does things and to consider different approaches – by different people, in a different way or even in a different location. There may even be activities that do not need to be done at all.

In general, social housing landlords are not examining their use of office space in detail and are not currently adopting flexible spacing strategies. One which has tried is Magna Housing Association.

Case study: Magna Housing Association

Magna has seen rapid growth in the last four years. Despite using two offices of some 12,500 square feet, it still needs more office space. However, many of the staff are in the office for no more than six hours in every 24 and Magna is, therefore, considering the introduction of hot-desking where office space can be booked together with improved computer facilities, mobile phones, pagers, e-mail, etc. The provision of such facilities, especially 'home computers', is considered to be particularly advantageous to development staff.

❑ 6.6 Moving towards a paperless office

The 'paperless office' is a concept that has been around for some time with only limited application in the social housing field. Knowledge Brokers' research for this Guide revealed that even when RSLs had the technology available to move towards a paperless office, they often adopted a 'belt and braces' approach of keeping paper documents which had also been computerised. Copies were often made of e-mail messages as if to validate them.

Checklist of steps for moving to a paperless office

- ❑ E-mail should replace memos.
- ❑ All essential business documents to be electronic documents.
- ❑ Problems in using e-mail must be reported and solved promptly.
- ❑ Redesign processes and systems to replace old ones completely.
- ❑ Systems must be in place to avoid internal junk e-mail.
- ❑ Systems must preserve confidentiality.
- ❑ Staff should be strongly discouraged from printing messages.
- ❑ Monitoring should be in place to ensure that everyone maintains the service response times which have been set for aspects of work.

Case study: The potential of the paperless office – BT

An organisation of 600 people has completely converted to electronic working. Communication is by e-mail not by letter or memo. Staff have been promised that their heads of department would respond to their e-mails within 12 hours. The average response time is in fact 3-4 hours and 98% of all responses are made within the 12 hour target. The remaining 2% are primarily delayed because some senior managers were abroad at the time. The introduction of electronic working has resulted in a radically different organisational structure with only two layers of management instead of four. More people work from home, meeting others only when that is needed.

CHAPTER 7

TECHNOLOGICAL REQUIREMENTS

This chapter describes the technology which underpins teleworking and other new ways of working. It begins by describing developments in computer technology and then looks at other teleworking tools.

❑ 7.1 Personal computers

A personal computer is an essential part of a teleworker's tool kit. It can be used for preparing reports, analysing and processing statistical data and producing leaflets. A computer can also gain access to information held on other computers around the world via a modem, ISDN line or leased line and use the internet.

Teleworkers may well find a laptop or notebook computer more useful than a desktop computer. Laptops and notebooks are portable and can be operated using batteries or mains supply. This enables teleworkers to use them wherever they need. Housing staff can communicate with the social housing provider's corporate databases, such as rent accounting, housing management and maintenance databases, via a modem (see below), ISDN line or leased line. A housing officer could give applicants an immediate assessment of their rehousing chances. A repairs inspector could issue an order for works to be done and give a copy there and then to the tenant.

Laptop computers perform the same functions as a desktop computer. The main disadvantage of laptop and notebook computers are their small screens and keyboards. One option is to use a docking system which links a laptop to a desktop computer. This is less costly than having two separate machines and removes the need to transfer data from one machine to the other.

❑ 7.2 Client servers

There is a shift away from using mainframe computers linked to a number of 'dumb' computer terminals – merely screens which replicate data on the central mainframe computer – to client server technology. The server is a central computer which contains information and links to other computers which are called clients, usually personal computers. The PCs gain access to the server via a network. A PC can, therefore, use data and programs on the server and also use its own software, data and programs.

In a typical teleworking arrangement, the server would be located at the employing organisation's head office, teleworkers' PCs would be the clients and ISDN would provide the network linking the two together. Networking technologies such as modems and extranets are now widely used to enable PCs to share programs and data.

Client servers have become more widespread with the advent of the pentium chip which has greatly enhanced the power and speed of PCs. In addition, servers allow a number of people in an organisation to use **groupware** – a software package which enables a number of geographically dispersed people to work simultaneously on the same file or document.

❑ 7.3 Electronic mail (e-mail)

E-mail is electronic messaging, which may be either a corporate system such as Microsoft Exchange (which would also be used by the people working within the organisation as an additional means of communicating on a day to day basis) or may be provided by a public internet service provider (ISP) such as Demon or BT (whereby the organisation may have a specific e-mail address with a series of accounts which can be used for mailing a specific teleworker.)

E-mail is the key to successful teleworking. It is cheaper, quicker and easier to use than a fax. Every e-mail user has an unique e-mail address. This makes it an ideal method of communication for teleworking.

Commonly used e-mail networks are 'store and forward' systems. This means that the person receiving the message does not have to be working on their computer to receive the message. Instead, the message is stored on the system until the recipient logs on to check their e-mail.

E-mail is a good way of transmitting information that needs to be reworked by the recipient. Most e-mail systems provide an electronic filing system for messages. E-mail messages may contain numbers of files as attachments. This allows one person to send another an e-mail message and attach a number of documents or other files from their computer.

The capabilities of e-mail have improved significantly with the widespread use of a common format (Adobe's portable document format or PDF). This format allows a document to be transmitted electronically. In doing so, it retains its formatting, typefaces and graphics without compatibility problems, irrespective of the hardware or software used by the sender and recipient.

There are also plans to launch a network of satellites to provide low cost e-mail services across the globe. Using an inexpensive compact receiver, about the size of a laptop computer, users will be able to send e-mail messages for the equivalent of a few pence. This will bring e-mail services within the reach of many small and medium sized organisations. Comparatively low cost providers of e-mail services such as CompuServe also provide flexible communications capabilities and are easy to use.

For mobile workers, new technologies exist to allow these employees to access their e-mail whilst in transit.

❑ 7.4 Fax machine

A fax capability is a vital piece of equipment for a teleworker. A fax enables the transmission of documents and simple pictures in seconds. It provides a good way of getting short, sometimes urgent, messages from one place to another.

It has some advantages over e-mail in that a fax message is readily visible and does not require the person receiving the message to have their PC on. It also has some disadvantages. For example, a fax message is not in a computer readable form and so may need re-processing. However, most modern computers (provided they have a fax card or fax modem) can transmit fax messages from one computer to another and so overcome this.

Many fax machines have additional features. They can be combined with a telephone and answering machine. They can be combined with a printer and scanner.

A fax can be programmed to send information overnight to take advantage of cheaper telephone tariffs or to send documents to another time zone. A telecommunications service even allows an employer to send the same faxed message to all home-based employees.

Mobile workers can use fax cards in mobile telephones to transmit and receive faxes whilst in transit. Comparatively low cost cards can be purchased for insertion in to mobile phones, which enable a PC to be linked to a mobile phone to enable the loading and downloading of data on the mobile phone network. This enables a teleworker to access their e-mail, send faxes, access rent accounts, etc, when, say, at a tenant's home without the need to access a traditional landline telephone.

❑ 7.5 The internet

The internet is a public network which provides users with a low cost, easy way of transmitting and accessing data without the need for bespoke corporate networks to accommodate remote workers. This enables workers, for approximately £10 per month, to send their e-mail and to send/receive documents from either their organisation or, if appropriate, from other agencies or even tenants. Internet service providers (ISPs) include Demon and BT.

The internet is a worldwide network of computer networks connected to each other by telecommunications links. It is made up of individuals and organisations who have decided to share information in a giant, interconnected open system.

ISDN (see below) will enable greater exploitation of the internet as it will make available a wider menu of multimedia and is speedier.

Currently the main uses of the internet are communication via e-mail (see above), plus information gathering and marketing. The marketing potential of the internet has attracted many business users seeking to exploit a worldwide market via cyberspace. A distinguishing feature of marketing through the internet is that it is **interactive**.

❑ 7.6 Mobile telephones and pagers

Mobile telephones enable teleworkers to stay in touch with their head office and customers wherever a signal is available. Most parts of the United Kingdom are now within range of the major mobile 'phone networks but social housing organisations, operating in some remote areas, should check before providing staff with mobiles.

Mobile telephones can be cheap to buy but can be expensive to run. However, tariffs are coming down as a result of a mass market and increased competition. Regulatory intervention has also meant that the ability to tie people into agreements has been constrained. Large users, such as some social housing organisations, can negotiate special deals with the providers of air time. One alternative is a cordless telephone. This allows teleworkers to receive or make calls within about a 60 metre radius of the office base unit.

If a mobile telephone is not cost effective, pagers may be an option. These store messages or offer a voice mail service. Many systems have no charges apart from the initial purchase price. Instead, the caller is charged – which might make pagers an attractive option for some teleworkers.

❑ 7.7 Modems

Modems allow data to be transmitted over standard telephone lines so that one computer can communicate with another. Modems can be internal (built into a computer) or can be external (added on separately).

Modems cut out the need and cost of printing a document, inserting it into a fax machine and sending it to another. The recipient can load the file sent by the remote computer (via the modem) straight into the recipient's computer memory ready for use, thereby eliminating the need to re-type it.

Modems also allow a computer to access the internet, provided the user has subscribed to a suitable internet service provider, where any user can find information on a variety of subjects and communicate with any other internet user worldwide.

❑ 7.8 Networks

A number of computers can be linked together to share data and communicate as a local area network (LAN). The computers are linked to each other with cables between PCs or via a microwave link. This allows computer users to be on a different site but still be linked to the same computer system (via their own PC) shared by the rest of the organisation. A user can still use their own PC in 'stand alone' mode. A wide area network (WAN) allows computers to communicate with each other electronically within different organisations and across large distances.

❑ 7.9 Printers

Despite the advances in e-mail, few offices in the social housing sector are completely paper free. Although staff may be able to communicate with colleagues via e-mail, they may still need to communicate with external customers on paper. So a teleworker will need a printer.

A wide variety of printers exist – ink jet or laser, colour or black and white, free standing or part of another device such as a fax. The choice will depend on the type and volume of the material the teleworker needs to print. One printer can be shared by a number of computers to save costs.

Mobile workers working on customer premises can use small, low cost printers to print forms and agreements on site – thereby eliminating the need for teleworkers to carry cases of paper documents and providing a highly responsive service to tenants.

❑ 7.10 Scanners

A scanner (sometimes known as a document imaging system) converts type and images on paper, including photographs, logos and diagrams into computer-based images which can be displayed on a screen. These images can then be edited and inserted into documents in other software programs. It may not be necessary for every teleworker to have a scanner. Instead, a central office could scan documents and then e-mail them to the teleworker.

❑ 7.11 Software

A number of software packages already exist which teleworkers can use. In addition, some organisations which have introduced teleworking have had specific software packages developed to meet their own requirements.

Teleworkers are likely to need an integrated software package containing the following:

- word processing – the most widely used function and most essential;
- spreadsheets – for the large scale manipulation of numbers and statistical analysis;
- databases – for storing data in a structured way;
- desktop publishing – for the design of pages, newsletters etc;
- graphics – for the creation and manipulation of images such as logos;

- presentation – for combining text, graphics and images in a series of slides, eg, for training sessions;
- diary and time/calendar – to aid time management;
- computer supported co-operative working (CSCW) tools or groupware – to aid collaborative working; and
- access to the internet – where corporate e-mail is not in use, the internet is an ideal substitute.

Staff within an organisation should use the same software. Without this, the free flow of data between teleworkers and their head office will be hampered, because work in one piece of software cannot always be translated into another.

❑ 7.12 Technical support

Teleworkers will need to be able to call upon expert technical support. If their equipment is not functioning properly they will not be able to work until it is fixed. Some larger social housing landlords already have their own in-house IT expert. Others often rely upon the supplier of their hardware or software for technical advice and support, or have a maintenance agreement with a third party to provide support and fix problems. The advantage of external support is that assistance can be available on a 24 hour, seven day a week basis. Whichever method is used, teleworkers must be able to get the advice they need very quickly, possibly even having priority over office-based staff. This may mean negotiating service agreements – in respect of hardware and perhaps software – with service providers in the same geographical area as the teleworker.

Teleworking is dependent on a sound telecommunications infrastructure – therefore the corporate architecture must be sufficiently robust to provide good response times and also be adequately secure. Depending on the size of the housing organisation, and its geographical distribution, the telecommunications support in terms of fixing PCs, etc, can be delivered from the centre through help-desks, through home visits or through a maintenance contract with a third party service provider.

❑ 7.13 Telecommunications lines

In the past, telephone lines going from local exchanges through the national and international networks, have been used for moving text and data between computers. However, there are problems when graphics, video and images need to be transported, as the lines do not have enough 'bandwidth' capacity. Transmission can be slow and erratic.

Technological solutions to this problem include optical fibre or ISDN links.

■ Optical fibre

Optical fibre cables are tiny strands of glass which carry messages as pulses of light. They provide broad bandwidth that enables the low cost transmission of fast clear video, voice and data. Optical fibres are installed at main telecommunication junction points and exchanges in the UK. It is estimated that optical fibre links carry more than 90% of UK communications. The problem is that, in most cases, the signal still runs into the old copper cables between the telephone exchange and work/home, and then slows down.

■ Integrated services digital network (ISDN)

An integrated services digital network (ISDN) is a new type of telephone line which allows very large amounts of data to be transmitted from the sender to the recipient. ISDN can not only transmit voice, fax and data but also sophisticated graphics and video – containing too much data for a standard telephone line.

Modems take the digital information from a computer and convert it into an analogue format to send to the local telephone exchange. Most local exchanges in Britain are now digital, so the data is translated back into a digital format for sending down the main digital networks. It is converted back into an analogue format when it reaches the local exchange at its destination. At the final stage of its journey, the modem at the receiver's end reconverts the information back into a digital format for the receiver's computer. However, ISDN can replace the need for modems.

ISDN enables much better and faster communication between linked computers. It means that complete files or reports can be transmitted in seconds rather than the minutes which elapse when using conventional e-mail. ISDN can save costs – calls are at the same rate as the standard network but the quicker time they take means they cost less. ISDN can only work through telephone exchanges which work on the digital system. Not every exchange in the United Kingdom has yet been converted but this should soon be the case. ISDN operates to worldwide standards and so can be used not only in the UK but overseas as well.

Standard telephone lines are analogue; mobile phones can be either digital or analogue – most nowadays are digital. Digital is merely standard 0 & 1s which are rapidly switched on and off and is the means by which computers operate/communicate. ISDN is digital.

There are three means by which a teleworker can access a corporate network.

Public switch telephone network (PSTN) where the maximum connection speed is 115,200 bits per second with data compression (this is a telecommunications 'industry standard'). The achievement of this speed is rare because the assumption is that every file that is transmitted compresses to its ideal which in practice is rare. However, the physical connection speed is typically 28,800 or 33,600 or the latest is 56,000 because these are the standard modem speeds – but these are getting faster all the time.

Integrated services digital network (ISDN) has two channels both of which are digital. These are capable of 64,000 bits per second (this too is a telecommunications industry standard speed). This is much faster (even without data compression) and the main advantage is that it does not suffer from the noise problems which analogue suffers which causes transmission over analogue to be slower and less stable than digital. ISDN is a more expensive form of transmission but its cost is typically well within the reach of most social housing providers.

Global services network (GSN) is digital and is accessed via a mobile phone. This network is capable of transmitting data at the same speeds as ISDN but because of interference during transmission – that which is typically experienced by any digital mobile phone – in practice the data transmission speed is 9600 (current telecommunications industry standard). This is quite slow for data transmission but it is likely to increase to14,400 next year. Meanwhile, it is usually quite pragmatic for e-mail and sometimes for accessing corporate databases.

Prior to deciding to embark on remote working, it is advisable to conduct a short study into the technical capability of the corporate telephone network, as a result of which it may be necessary to make some upgrades. It is also imperative to evaluate the security of the network and to make upgrades if appropriate.

Where an organisation is not able to upgrade its network, it may be feasible to use an internet services provider (ISP) to create an external e-mail account for the organisation, into which documents and mail can be both sent and retrieved. It should be remembered, however, that an ISP is a public network and although the e-mail, theoretically, is private, hackers could access it – so it should be used for information which is not overly sensitive.

❑ 7.14 Telephone services and costs

Most telephone exchanges in the United Kingdom are already, or soon will be, digital. This allows teleworkers to make use of a number of useful telephone services. These include caller display, call waiting, three way conferencing and call diversion.

This last service can be very useful. It enables calls to be diverted from a teleworker's direct line in the office to their home equipment without the caller being aware that this is happening. Enquiries can be dealt with immediately, rather than a message being left which will be dealt with sometime later.

An answering service held on the local exchange with a personalised recorded message has advantages too. The user can check her or his messages from any telephone linked to a digital exchange.

Messaging services on mobile telephones allow messages to be left for mobile workers when they are on customer premises and, therefore, have switched their phones off.

Consideration should be given to installing a separate telephone line specifically for a teleworker's work activities. This should be a digital line if the teleworker is likely to be using ISDN and other advanced technology.

At present, telephone tariffs are falling. A social housing organisation may well be able to negotiate a particularly good rate for the installation and running costs of its teleworkers' lines. Costs can also be saved through the careful design of the organisation's telecommunications system.

The internet can also provide a means of communication for teleworkers. Although the current quality of internet transmission is not as clear as a standard telephone, it is a significantly cheaper method of making international calls – as charges for access to the internet are at local rates.

The optimum integration of teleworking within an organisation – whether it be homeworking or in-transit working – is to interface with technology, people and processes with those operating within a call centre.

This relationship, particularly when combined with an outbound dialling capability, facilitates good communication in the areas of work management (eg, whereby the call centre staff can schedule appointments with the teleworker through the use of work management software).

Teleworkers would be equipped with either handheld devices or laptop computers whereby they are able to dial into the corporate systems (eg, to retrieve electronic mail, to access up-to-date account records for tenants, etc). This type of access would be on an intermittent basis as work dictates. These databases may be held on mainframe or client server technology depending on the configuration of the organisation's network.

Tenants may also have access to corporate databases via, say, kiosks on estates through which they may, for example, update their own tenant records or access rent information, depending on the policies of the organisation.

Tenants wishing to make specific enquiries may have a single point of contact with the organisation through the organisation's call centre.

Case study: Thames Valley Housing Association – Teleworking

Thames Valley Housing Association manages around 5000 homes, scattered over 30 local authority areas in West London and five Thames Valley counties, from a single HQ office based in Twickenham, West London. It employs around 100 staff and is developing around 400 new homes a year.

It decided to introduce teleworking for its outreach housing management officers following a major review of its business operations.

The Association was aware that 20% of housing management officers' time was spent in their cars – partly as a result of 'unnecessary' routine visits to HQ each day. This was also true of maintenance surveyors and other staff who were required to visit tenants and leaseholders in their own homes. A further issue was the duplication of effort and visits caused by specialist functional working. Three or even four officers may have needed to visit an estate to resolve a problem.

Ironically, as more local authority partners demanded a 'local service presence', existing local offices were under-utilised and not cost-effective.

The Association was disappointed with this, as it wished to enhance face-to-face contact with customers.

Finally, the Association's HQ was staffed to maximum capacity. Any further staff growth would have involved highly expensive relocation.

Thames Valley held a series of successful residents' conferences at which the key issues highlighted were the need to improve the telephone service – the main means by which tenants contacted the organisation – and resident consultation. The Association employed PPRC to undertake a customer values survey which asked tenants and leaseholders what they valued about services and how satisfied they were with actual service delivery.

The Association then undertook a major business process re-engineering exercise, where frontline staff were invited to reassess and improve the Association operations.

As a result, Thames Valley introduced both generic working and teleworking for six housing management staff, plus a service centre. The new approach has been 'live' since 1 April 1998.

The service centre differs from a standard call centre in terms of the operations it performs. It is located in a customer service department which also includes a tenancy management team. The service centre aims to provide an immediate response to the vast majority of telephone enquiries – by access to the necessary technological and professional support. Following intensive training – and with support from the tenancy management team – the eight service centre operators can:

- handle all standard housing management enquiries – complicated and difficult enquiries are referred to the tenancy management team;
- order maintenance work in response to telephone requests through the use of diagnostic software;

- update tenancy and rent records;
- control operational officers' diaries and make appointments; and
- pass messages and instructions to operational officers.

Four frontline operational officers cover discreet geographical patches and are provided with laptops and modems. At the start of each day they consult their electronic diary which lists their appointments for the day ahead. They can access tenancy and rent records from the Association's Context database via e-mail via their mobile phone or by using a freephone number from tenants' homes. They can also 'dial in' from tenants' homes by using their modems. After each appointment, they contact the service centre to confirm their whereabouts. At the end of each day, they spend around 30 minutes 'mopping up' details of each interview and inputting data to the Context database via e-mail.

Operational officers have also been trained to handle maintenance request assessments and welfare and benefits advice. They visit the office one day a week for team meetings and 'one-to-one' discussions with managers.

Operational officers are backed up by two regional officers, of greater seniority, who handle the more difficult appointments and spend, on average, two days per week in the office. The work of operations and regional officers is, in turn, co-ordinated by a senior operations officer who reports to an operations manager.

The Association has introduced hot-desking for teleworking staff, thus freeing up scarce office accommodation.

A Tenancy Management Team provides specialist advice and administrative support to service centre and outreach operations staff.

A Client Services team monitors the effectiveness of operations and service centre staff, and provides a resource to the operations staff by way of assistance with special needs housing, tenant participation and Best Value.

Teleworking required changes in staff job descriptions, but no increase in salaries. Negotiations with trade unions were successful and involved matters such as coffee and 'comfort breaks' and compensation for the loss of free car parking. Improved health and safety control resulted from improved IT contact with off-site workers.

From the customer point of view, the system worked as follows. The customer rings the service centre requesting an appointment, where an operator accesses the relevant operations officer's computerised diary. The service centre will firstly determine whether a visit is required or whether the matter can be dealt with over the telephone. The service centre will also determine the urgency of the matter – and decide whether the tenant can be visited as part of the operations officer's weekly round or whether a special visit is required. An appointment which suits the customer and fits with the operations officer's schedule is then selected. The onus is on the Association to visit the customer rather than the converse.

The switch to teleworking led to the following costs:

- 6 laptops at £2,500 each = £15,000;
- 6 modems at £400 each = £2,400; and
- training for operations officers on maintenance matters = £1,500.

These costs were offset against the following savings:

- 4 car parking spaces in a multi-storey car park adjacent to the office at £900 per year each = £3,600; and
- replacement of 6 obsolete desktop PCs at £1000 each = £6000.

The direct short-term cost of introducing teleworking was, therefore, only £9,300.

The introduction of teleworking will actually save the Association an estimated £750,000 over three years, by relieving it of having to move its main office and having to set up regional offices to meet local authority requirements for a 'local service presence'.

Efficiency gains have also been achieved. The reduction in travelling time for operations officers will enable them to 'add value' to their service by freeing up time for intensive 'Housing Plus' and resident participation work

Service delivery model

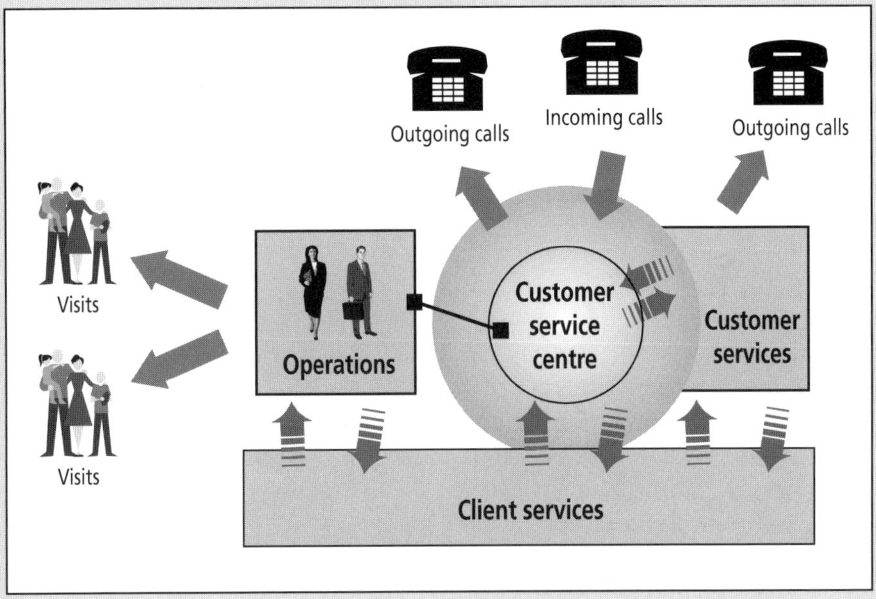

CHAPTER 8

THE FUTURE OF TECHNOLOGY AND SOCIAL HOUSING

This chapter looks at future trends in technology and the use of office space, and considers their potential impact on the work of social housing organisations. It provides practical examples of what can be achieved and at what will be achievable in the not too distant future.

❑ 8.1 The future office

It may be that people will look back nostalgically to the days when they went to the office between 9 am and 5 pm to work. Current and future opportunities which communications technology present to organisations could mean that offices – as we understand them – and traditional working hours, could become largely obsolete.

The concept of an office was introduced as a direct result of the need for the central processing of information and tasks. In other words, the need for large numbers of people to work together required a highly disciplined regime with fixed hours, clear separation of home and office and a localised commuting infrastructure. All of this followed from the inflexibility of information flows and was developed as a direct response to the relatively high costs involved if the information on which people were to work was not centralised at a single place. Information was paper based, word of mouth was important. The whole organisation functioned as a cohesive whole requiring proximity since the greater the distance information was to travel, the longer the time it would take and the more it would cost.

The advent of information technologies – including greater telecommunications infrastructures to the hardware, and software which can make use of this enhanced infrastructure – has reduced the time and cost of the transfer of information to the point where it is no longer a major inhibitor requiring centralised processing. As a result the office has lost its main reason for being.

Evidence suggests that the costs of an office approach, formerly lower than the costs of a decentralised system, are now actually higher. Consequently, as firms strive to improve their efficiency, cost cutting will inevitably result in classical office structures being wholly or partly replaced by teleworking, which is cheaper and may result in higher productivity.

❑ 8.2 Predictions for 2000 and beyond

The next 10 to 15 years will see further increases in the pace of change in the field of communications. Organisations which have just recently begun to consider the benefits of e-mail could, in a few years, be holding video conferences in virtual rooms.

Over this 10 to 15 year period it is predicted that:

- an increasing number of people of working age will be computer literate;
- video conferencing – in various forms – will have replaced a good part of physical travel;
- employees and members of the public will have enormous computing power readily available to them;
- people will be able to carry most of the IT items that they require for a given job;
- computers will be able to understand and be operated by everyday spoken language;
- it will be possible to automatically translate information from one language to another;
- there will be greater integration of everyday technology such as televisions, PCs, home appliances and games for work and pleasure;
- offices will be fully computerised with automatic data sorting, filtering and decision support being widely available; and
- organisations will be using networking (eg, the internet) to conduct business functions and gather information.

In more general terms, the 21st century will see office working change to a more flexible regime, with much more fluid patterns of work, all supported by communications technology. Offices could evolve to become more like clubs – a place where people with mutual interests come together to share knowledge and information in more informal contexts. While the focus will remain the **functions** of the organisation, the office will represent a place to take stock of situations, a place where collective decision-making and ideas are generated, and where a certain level of socialisation among colleagues will occur. Of course, offices will still exist in the next century – but they will be used in new ways. They will be specifically designed to enable interaction between people and will be based on a much more social and less time dependent way of life. The future office is likely to be less hierarchical and more democratic, flexible and dynamic.

The social housing sector is not likely to escape this trend. Indeed, its requirements are very conducive to the application of technology. Since the bulk of this Guide has covered teleworking, this chapter will instead focus on some of the other areas in which an organisation will face change.

❑ 8.3 Technology for customer service

Traditionally the two main entities which make up the social housing sector – local authorities and housing associations – have had to submit information to lengthy scrutiny before it can be used. These processes have generally not been rationalised, nor created with customer satisfaction as a central goal. Increasingly, however, social housing providers are focusing on customer satisfaction.

But what is it that the customer actually wants? What if the answer lies in allowing the customer to define his/her own service while the organisation focuses on delivering their requirements.

How can technology enable this to happen?

A young couple who are currently tenants of a RSL are expecting a baby. Ideally, they require slightly larger living accommodation, preferably in the same area. One morning they walk over to an electronic kiosk which, after asking them for some basic personal information so as to be able to find their file on the database, begins offering them options. They select 'Transfer request' from the menu, bringing them to the relocation system which already displays information on their current home in part of the screen. Through a series of simple touch-screen choices they input all of the information required, including that they require a larger space, preferably in the same area as their current residence. The screen explains the landlord's transfer policy and procedures. The system also currently checks their eligibility for a transfer – checking rent payments, size of property etc.

If they meet the RSL's criteria, the kiosk then presents suitable and available accommodation fitting the requirements made. A single screen shows a property which is available, together with some general information, such as the exact address, and a picture of the property (from the outside). They decide to look further by pressing on 'Further Information' and are presented with a menu offering the following:

- local amenities;
- local transport;
- virtual walk through the residence; and
- special issues.

After having reviewed all the information, they turn to the 'Local Information' option to be informed that there is one nearby park and two local childrens' play areas. They are also informed that the nearest hospital with full maternity facilities is St. Elsewhere, a 10 minute walk or 4 minute ride on the number 123 bus. There are also three schools serving the area. A map of the area shows where all of these facilities are in relation to the property.

Deciding that this is where they wish to transfer to, they use the kiosk to print out all the information in a report that they can take away. They also use the kiosk to make an appointment with a representative of the RSL to discuss the matter further. They pick a date and time on which they will both be available and which is suitable to one of the local area representatives whose schedule they are reviewing for a slot. A confirmation that the representative will be visiting them to discuss the matter on the following Wednesday at 5 pm is also printed out by the kiosk.

So what is required for this to be a reality? Actually, very little that is not already available within the social housing sector and certainly nothing new as far as technology is concerned. The kiosk is possible, the interface to the user is a simple graphical user interface which can be created with a number of off-the-shelf, easy to use programs by anyone trained to do so or by a company specialising in this sort of work. Any graphics presented are the result of new data being integrated to existing data entry processes, themselves making use of available technologies which can be used in the field, such as digital cameras. A 'virtual walk through' of the accommodation is nothing more than the result of some digital pictures of the property taken the last time the property was surveyed and input into the central database of properties. Information on local amenities and transport is accessed from existing databases in the UK. This is similarly the case for 'Local Information', collected by a search agent embedded in the kiosk software, itself commercially available and very easily implemented. Access to the diaries of local representatives implies that these personnel make available part (or all) of their schedules through the system. This is not difficult if such schedules are already computer based, with representatives working with laptops from wherever they are. Printing, the final piece of the puzzle, is very easily included with the kiosk functions.

The benefits of such an approach are numerous. To start with, the couple have undertaken a great deal of the preliminary sorting work which is currently undertaken by social housing sector representatives, thus saving a great deal of time and effort, if not expense. When the couple does meet the RSL's representative they will need a shorter interview and it will be focused on the specific actions to be taken, rather than on defining what the options are or what properties are available. Before the meeting, the couple will also have the opportunity of looking at the property as they will know the address. The system can even be implemented where an on-site visit is arranged through the kiosk, or, alternatively, the meeting could be scheduled to occur at the actual property in question so that the RSL representative can walk them through it and thereby be on hand to answer questions as they arise.

Equally important is the fact that the couple will have been involved in the process and from the outset will have an active role in their destiny. It is a process activated by them and for which they become responsible. They make the appointment and will thus be much more likely to keep it. They take an active role in identifying the suitability of the property.

If there is any difficulty it is in the retrieval of the data to be presented. However, all of this data is likely to already reside on computers somewhere. The information needs simply to be made accessible to the computer(s) with which the kiosk communicates through the telephone or similar device. The personal data is available within the social housing infrastructure, it simply needs to be stored and delivered more effectively. Information on available properties matching the criteria specified by the couple is the result of a relatively simple search conducted on databases which currently already exist. Checking whether the couple are eligible for a transfer according to the RSL's criteria is the result of checking their details using a computerised allocations and transfers system.

Once such a system is available, the way in which it is delivered is flexible. A kiosk is nothing more than a readily available interface to a host of organised data. In time other forms of interaction will also be available. For example, if the couple have a home computer and a modem, one can replace 'kiosk' with 'internet web page'. Soon internet access will be available through television sets, much as access to Teletext is at the moment. Then replace 'kiosk' with 'television set'. The important point is that once the infrastructure is there, the delivery mechanism can be adjusted to fit the customer. In all likelihood, the service will be provided by all three interfaces – kiosk, home computer and TV – simultaneously, allowing users to choose which one they prefer at a given moment.

But let us continue with the couple with the transfer request.

On the way back from the kiosk they stop and have a look at the outside of the property they are considering. A woman is coming out of the flat next door so they stop and tell her what they are planning, and that they may soon be neighbours. During the discussion which follows the couple are told that the flat on the other side of the one they are considering is inhabited by a group of rather loud youths. Decidedly worried about this they make their way home and call the housing service centre to report on what they found. The service centre customer representative pulls up all relevant information on the couple (including their latest requests via the kiosk) in response to a few questions used to identify them. The representative is then able to provide more information on their options.

The customer representative then asks the couple for further information on the alleged disturbances which are the cause of the change in their plans. All the information obtained is input into an appropriate incident report which also prompts the questions to be asked. Once key information is collected, the report is logged and passed to the RSL personnel who are responsible for acting upon it.

Again, all of the information and technology to turn this into a reality is currently available. The interface and information available on the kiosk is also available to customer representatives at head office or call centres through their PCs. Information on the couple's activities at the kiosk only an hour earlier is available because all records are updated in real time and the information is immediately available throughout the system. Since the information would include not only the search they conducted, but also the response they obtained, the representative is able to review the situation with the couple over the phone.

The representative was also able to easily point and click on her or his interface so that the information could be sent by post. Once the 'send info by post' option has been activated the system itself could see to it that the relevant information is automatically printed, put in a folder and sent to the waiting couple. This can be as manually intensive or as automated as the organisation desires – the entire printing and mailing process can be automated if throughput levels warrant it, or could alternatively be outsourced to a cost competitive supplier of such services.

But what of the incident report? Technically, this is another easily accessible process to which the customer representative has access, since sometimes people do call specifically to report problems – whether a burst water pipe, a broken window or, as in this case, a difficulty with neighbours. The interface to the representative provides space for information to be input, as well as prompting the specific questions to be asked to obtain the information required for the incident to be pursued. Once the relevant information is included, the incident report is sent on its way. As far as the customer representative is concerned, her job is finished. But what happens to the report?

This is where we can look, from the management perspective, at how technology can be applied to make the actual running, management and performance of the entire social housing infrastructure more effective.

❑ 8.4 Technology for decisions

Operational decisions taken in the social housing sector may affect a range of operations and, therefore, other managers. However, the infrastructure on which they rely for the information used in making decisions often impacts upon the quality of decisions made.

In the example of the transfer request described above, if the customer representative does not pass on the information about the alleged disturbance to a case officer to investigate or to the representative who is due to see the couple, the quality of the RSL's service is adversely affected. Existing tenants may be inconvenienced and potential tenants deterred from moving in.

What happens after the customer service representative enters the incident report onto their computer?

The report is logged into a database. However, this is not the first report on this residence, two others have been logged in the past month alone. As a result an automatic review of the situation – based on some simple rules – is automatically undertaken by the computer. To start with it checks the origin of the reports; is it just one person constantly complaining, or is it several? Are there outstanding incident reports on those reporting this incident, perhaps logged by those being reported this time round? A local feud perhaps? A host of questions can be asked, each with a particular implication which assists in forming a picture of what is going on.

As it turns out, in this case at least, each report is from a different source. Dates are then cross checked to see if any two reports relate to the same incident and if the reports started in conjunction with any other particularly relevant event such as the arrival of new tenants. A host of such automatic checks are conducted on the data so as to arrive at a final picture of the situation. The information arrived at is then automatically e-mailed to an appropriate case officer to pursue.

The handling of such complaints thus becomes more efficient, as case officers are automatically presented with the information they require in the instances where action is required. Hence they focus on resolving the problem rather than on the identification of problems. Moreover, workload can be automatically distributed among existing staff, and based on experience, skills and workload. The person sent the e-mail dossier is then not only suitable for resolving the problem identified, but is also the most available to do so promptly.

This approach can be applied to many other areas such as the identification and dispatch of contractors to fix reported leaks or broken windows. In general, if anything is done on a repeated basis, then the decision-making process which underlies the action will also be occurring repeatedly. It is likely that the same checks and processes are being consistently applied each time, and can be automated – rendering the process more efficient and less costly, but also making it systematic and consistent.

Furthermore, complete records of activities are created. In the case of repairs, for example, a complete record of repairs can be automatically created and maintained for each property as the repairs are undertaken. This allows the possibility of focusing management time on the more difficult or more important aspects of service decision making. For example, the system could then flag anomalies to managers as they occur, such as if a given flat requires a new window an inordinate number of times over a given period. What is happening there? The system points out where attention needs to be focused. At a higher level still, the entire financial reporting of maintenance costs would become available in real time for review and consideration when decisions are required.

This could be particularly helpful when locating suppliers, negotiating bulk discounts, assigning preferred contractors, etc. For example, knowing that on average a housing authority will require 4000 new windows in a given year will help when negotiating a contract with a supplier of these windows. The same applies to all other materials required in the maintenance of a given housing stock, including human resources. Contractors could similarly be integrated into the system so that orders for jobs are automatically generated. These would allow long-term service contracts to be more readily monitored, yielding potential savings and allowing close monitoring of the quality of service provided.

Another area of potential application is the identification, location and project management of new housing stock.

An integrated approach to the provision of housing will give rise to information flows which will make the process of increasing or refurbishing the housing stock more efficient. To start with, real-time monitoring of demand will, over time, enable the creation of databases from which better predictions of demand patterns can be made. At the same time, systems to allow the real-time monitoring of supply could provide the other side of the equation, making matching of overall demand and supply more consistent. Senior management would have at its disposal the infrastructure to see where things stood at any point in time, rather than having to rely on information which reflects how things stood at some point in the past, or which tries to extrapolate how things will stand in the near future, say pending completion of a number of on-going projects.

From this base infrastructure the social housing sector could then start to explore the application of information technologies to related areas, such as build project management, automated pricing and sourcing of the materials required in the building project, which itself could be integrated directly to the platforms used by architects and building engineers. Ultimately, the application of new technology evolves through constant development and upgrading, integrating new ideas and approaches as they develop and making use of technologies to provide practical solutions to the problems with which the social housing sector is faced.

But how realistic is this? The answer is that everything described in this chapter is technically feasible now.

❑ 8.5 What does the future hold for social housing organisations?

The housing organisations surveyed for this book anticipated that, by the millennium, their technology would embrace call centres, office systems including document scanning, document imaging and new housing workflow systems and computer systems able to alert staff and managers to problems. Over this period they will also be working towards integrating their IT systems. In essence, the social housing sector views the adoption of many of the things described in this chapter and throughout this Guide as feasible, if not outright inevitable.

To achieve this, housing organisations need to look long and hard at developments in technology and ways of adopting technology to fit their particular business needs. At present, despite some evidence of small scale adoption of technologies in social housing, there is as yet no large scale successful demonstration pilot or scheme from which the sector can learn. However, it is clear that other sectors are finding substantial benefits in both cost and quality of service by adopting technologies. 'Wait and see' and 'better to be second than first' cultures seem to be prevailing in social housing. Some managers have even concluded that technology is changing too rapidly at the moment and wish to wait a few years before taking action. This assumes that in a few years technological advance will have slowed or that by waiting they will be better placed in the future. But what will hold them off for a few more years at that point? The end result could be perpetual waiting and stagnation.

The longer one waits the harder the transition becomes and the less competitive the organisation is vis-à-vis both the economy as a whole and the sector specifically. The biggest loss to an organisation of not making better use of technology is not the foregone efficiency that could be achieved or indeed the extra value that it could provide to clients. The real cost comes from the inability to adapt and deliver new value added services as the underlying market itself changes. In essence, the real cost is in long-term viability of the organisation itself.

In closing, it is worth noting the specific benefits which the introduction of technologies can yield. A social housing organisation can **now** choose to become an organisation which encompasses a range of flexible working practices and technologies which can enable it to enjoy the following benefits:

- it need no longer be a fixed structure but instead can become a more fluid network of resources to be used according to need and irrespective of physical location;
- it can more easily form and reform teams for particular activities and projects;
- it can achieve a better service for customers by automating recurring tasks as well as provide services around the clock;
- it can minimise the disruptive effects of natural or man made disasters;
- it can achieve better results as employees are able to concentrate more on their job functions by avoiding the distraction of having to deal with tasks which are superfluous to the real value they should be adding;
- it can create increased staff loyalty by offering greater flexibility and creativity;
- it can reduce employees' time and money spent on commuting;
- it can save on office costs;
- it can enable staff to spend more time with tenants and other customers; and
- it can tap into wider, more skilled labour markets.

The next step is up to the social housing sector. Will it have the vision and foresight to make the right choices? The answer to that remains to be seen.

APPENDIX 1

HOMEWORKERS' EMPLOYMENT RIGHTS CHARTER

(From the National Group on Homeworking)

1. **Equal employment rights for homeworkers:**
   - The term 'employee' in UK employment protection legislation (EPCA, TURER, HSAWA) should be replaced by the term 'worker' as used in the Wages Act 1986
   - The term self-employed should be defined in an Act of Parliament
   - The term worker should be 'an all encompassing' term to cover all working relationships except those genuinely self-employed as defined by Parliament

2. **A basic floor of employment rights for all workers who are not genuinely self-employed. This would include:**
   - Eligibility and protection from day one of the employment relationship
   - All workers whether homeworkers, part time, temporary, casual and irrespective of their hours of work would be protected
   - A series of short term 'contracts' will be counted as continuous service for the purpose of accruing employment and social security rights and benefits
   - These rights would include: maternity benefits, sickness benefits, redundancy rights, unfair dismissal protection, pensions entitlements
     - Health and safety protection as laid down in: (HSAWA, COSHH, RIDDOR, and TURER)
     - Representation in that industry. All workers should have an automatic right to be represented by an Organisation of their own choosing, regardless of their workplace location

3. **Employer responsibility**
   - All workers should receive the basic floor of protection unless their employer can prove that they are genuinely self-employed
   - Responsibility for employment terms and conditions should exist throughout the sub-contracting chains in that industry

4. **Establishment of an Enforcement Agency**
   - This would operate on a regional level as a separate agency or as part of the Industrial Tribunal system or ACAS and work in consultation with representatives from homeworking organisations
   - The agency would look into claims of self-employment and represent workers who felt they had been wrongly classified as self-employed
   - Workers' complaints would be anonymous to protect them
   - This agency would have the power to make decisions and settle disputes on site
   - Inland Revenue and DSS would have to abide by these decisions

5. **Inland Revenue and DSS**
   - Reform of the tax and social security system in line with the proposals of this charter
   - Clear guidelines on making employment status rulings would be given to both these bodies by central government as well as internal guidelines for monitoring these decisions
   - These guidelines would be publicly available
   - Both agencies would have to abide by the decisions made by the enforcement agency

6. **International standards on homeworking as laid down by the International Labour Organisation and the European Community should be ratified.**

The National Group on Homeworking (NGH) can be contacted at:

Office 26
30-38 Dock Street
Leeds LS10 1JF.

Telephone 0113 245 4273.

APPENDIX 2

TRADE UNION GUIDELINES

❑ BIFU and MSF guidelines

According to the finance trade union BIFU, homeworkers have traditionally been a 'hidden workforce, often unseen and unrepresented' and employed in 'textiles, footwear, hosiery, toys and novelty assembly and general sorting and packaging'. But now finance-sector companies are also beginning to use homeworkers, or perhaps more accurately, teleworkers.

Advantages and disadvantages

The union accepts that there are advantages in teleworking for its members. These include the relief of not needing to commute to work and greater working flexibility. But it also believes there are a number of disadvantages, including the isolation of working from home and extra costs, such as heating and lighting expenses, which are not always borne by employers. BIFU is also concerned that teleworkers are sometimes put on different employment contracts, and therefore separated from their colleagues and union representation.

Consequences of teleworking

BIFU believes that trade union recruitment is made more difficult because it splits a work unit into individuals working in different places. Current estimates put the proportion of unionised homeworkers at less than 15 per cent of the total. And attempting to recruit teleworkers on a large scale will be expensive for the union. The agricultural workers union (NIJAAW), for example, which was forced to merge with the TGWU in 1982 because it faced bankruptcy, had expended much of its resources in trying to recruit ever-smaller numbers of farm workers in far-flung areas.

Moreover, even if a union is able to recruit teleworkers in significant numbers, it will find it difficult to organise meetings that they can easily attend. And as there is less contact with the union, teleworkers may increasingly see union membership as an irrelevance.

Negotiators' guidelines

Unions, however, accept that some of their members will want to, or will be pressurised to, work from home. Consequently, a number have produced guidelines for negotiators to use. Below we summarise the guidelines published by two finance-sector unions: BIFU and MSF.

■ BIFU negotiators' guidelines

1. All tele/homeworkers must be volunteers.
2. Equipment such as desk, chair, personal computer, paper, pens and telephone lines should be supplied by the company.
3. The company should pay the tele/homeworker rent for the room/rooms given over to use for work purposes.
4. Any additional insurance premiums incurred because of the equipment used for homeworking must be met by the company.
5. Assurances must be sought from the company that they have investigated whether or not the tenancy agreement or mortgage will be affected by the member of staff working from home.
6. All additional heating, lighting and power bills incurred by someone working from home should be met by the company.
7. No 'spy in the home' cameras or key-depression monitoring should be fitted to a homeworker's VDU.
8. A regular health and safety check should be carried out by both management and the union of the homeworkers' room in which the work is to be undertaken.
9. Teleworking should never be used as an alternative to adequate workplace or state childcare.
10. Management should ensure that each homeworker has the opportunity to meet and discuss issues appertaining to their work at least once a week.
11. All homeworkers' contracts should be collectively agreed between management and the union, thereby ensuring that individuals do not find their terms and conditions worsened in comparison to other staff.
12. An agreement between the union and management on both the type of work and the number of people who are teleworking should be signed before people start teleworking.
13. An agreement from management to disclose the name and address of any new teleworker to BIFU should be signed before a teleworking agreement is embarked upon.

■ MSF teleworking guidelines

MSF has produced a set of teleworking guidelines that address the problems teleworkers can face. These are as follows:

- teleworkers should be employees of an enterprise and not deemed self-employed;
- to avoid isolation, contracts of employment should require homeworkers periodically to attend the office;
- there should be a separate room available at home for teleworking, a separate telephone and payment for additional costs;
- there should be regular meetings between teleworkers and the provision of electronic mail and telephone links with other teleworkers, all to be provided at the employers' expense;
- there should be regular weekly liaison discussions between a teleworker and his or her supervisor/manager;
- teleworkers should enjoy the same rates of pay and employment benefits as office-based workers including childcare provision and family leave. They should be included in career-development and appraisal schemes including training opportunities;
- all computer equipment should be provided, paid for and serviced by the employer who will be responsible for installation and compliance with health and safety requirements. The employer should also accept legal responsibility for any accident or injury;
- health and safety advisors and trade union representatives should be able to visit teleworkers and there should be a defined number of working hours;
- teleworking should be voluntary with a right to return to working from the office.

■

❑ Homeworking and teleworking – a UNISON briefing

Definitions

Homeworking is "work done in the home for another person or for sale to another person," according to a TUC statement of 1978, expanded in 1985 to include outworking and people working partly from home and at home. The statement does not define homeworking in relation to occupations or whether the worker is self-employed or not.

Teleworking – there is no single accepted definition.

1. 'the use of computing and telecommunications technology to extend elements of the working environment beyond the traditional workplace.' *National Computing Centre*, 1992.
2. 'a significant proportion of work time to be spent away from the employers premises.' *British Telecom*, 1993;
3. 'individuals based at home for at least 50% of their working time.' *Employment Department*, 1993.

Growth

Teleworking is still a minority activity but gaining in popularity. Between 5% and 15% of companies currently employ at least a few teleworkers. The greatest number are found in the finance and service sectors. And, reflecting the geographical concentration of these industries, teleworkers are most likely to be employed in the South of England. Whereas originally the prime development was in retaining heavily trained professionals, the predominant emphasis now is to use telework in order to reduce costs.

Homeworking is most common in manufacturing and distribution, but is also found in new, as well as old, industries and in the service, as well as the manufacturing, sector. Industrial restructuring and new technology are leading to more homework (a threefold increase in recent years).

The International Labour Organisation and the European Union (with a working party on homework) are trying to improve the status of homeworkers. The ILO Conference in June 1996 discussed a Convention on homework.

Benefits for the employer

- Can reduce office costs, but savings may not be as great as anticipated as many home/teleworkers do not work permanently from home, therefore office space is still required.
- Can lead to improvements in productivity – fewer interruptions, fewer motivation problems, greater job satisfaction.
- Staff recruitment and retention may also improve. It can enable employees who are unable to travel to work to remain in or to obtain employment. People with disabilities can benefit, as can parents with young children.
- Employers can employ staff in other areas of the country where staff costs may be lower.
- Greater flexibility, especially if workers are employed on a contract basis, with pay reviews dependent upon market conditions.

- Possible reduced absenteeism. There may be reduced levels of stress, and mildly ill people deterred by the journey to work, will work at home.

Benefits for the employee

- Saving commuting time – improved quality of life, more free time for employee, no travel stress.
- Increased flexibility and autonomy over the working day
- People with childcare responsibilities are not deterred from remaining in the job market. N.B.: some schemes disqualify people with young children because of the possible distraction factor.

Barriers to teleworking

For the employer

- Management difficulties – fear of loss of face-to-face contact, difficulties with motivation and discipline, organisational structure not designed for home/teleworking.
- Start up costs – office furniture and equipment.

For the employee

- Social isolation (possibly solved by combination of office and home work).
- Exclusion from certain conditions of service.
- Limited to certain jobs (highly skilled or professional; 'back office', i.e. wp operators, data entry etc).
- Problems of communication – loss of motivation for home/teleworker.
- Low pay (where an employee is part of a reduction in costs of contracts awarded through privatisation and competitive tendering).
- Casualisation (where employees eventually become self-employed).
- De-skilling (where opportunities for a wider variety of work are limited).

Trade union views

Many unions accept that there are advantages to members in home/teleworking but are concerned at pressures that can be brought to bear to force people into what could be a difficult employment environment.

Trade unions reflect the employees' concerns listed above. Unions are also concerned about the potential for cheap and highly exploitable labour, discrimination, extra stress on people juggling home and family life, and the possible lack of childcare facilities.

Example of a checklist for negotiating arrangements with employers

- Should always be voluntary.
- Should be employees (with full employment rights) not self-employed sub-contractors.
- Should operate from a separate room in the home, examined by qualified health & safety experts.
- Regular opportunities for workers to meet each other, as well as office-based colleagues.
- Should have access to electronic mail and telephone links.
- Should be assigned a particular manager who would ensure regular contact.
- Should have same rates of pay and other employment benefits as office-based workers.
- Should be included in career development programme of organisation – all equipment to be supplied and maintained by employer.
- Financial arrangements in place to cover extra costs, e.g. lighting, heating etc.
- Employers to be responsible for health & safety, H&S visits to be regular.
- Home workers should have their own representatives on organisation's health & safety committees.
- Home/teleworkers should enjoy the same rights as other workers to join trade unions and have their own representatives.
- Employees who transfer from office to home-based working should be entitled to a trial period and should have a right to return to previous arrangements. All workers should be entitled to an annual review of arrangements.

Typical contents of home/teleworking scheme

Pilot study
Criteria for selection of home/teleworkers
  Home life
  Personality of individual
  Type of work
Employee obligations
Management obligations
  Trade union representation
  Contact with office
  Career development
Pay and conditions

Practical details

Accommodation
Planning regulations incl mortgage implications
Tax
Insurance
Equipment to be provided
Security provisions
Health & Safety

Often accompanied by a Code of Practice

Employee schemes

Birmingham City Council – proposed scheme (Aug 1996)
British Gas Service – home start/home-based working agreement
British Telecommunications Plc – teleworking guidelines for managers
Camden (employed a Homeworking Officer – late 1980s)
Co-operative Bank
Digital Equipment Corporation – homeworking policy since 1983
Enfield Borough – Revenue Homeworkers project
Hackney – Homeworking strategy
Kent County Council – pilot telecentre working in August 1995
Leicester City – outworker policy/campaign in late eighties
Lothian Regional Council
Oxfordshire County Council's Flexiplace scheme
Surrey County Council – telecentre pilot to be run from September 1996
Wellcome Foundation – homeworking guidelines

Community support

Homeworker support groups in various London Boroughs. Other examples in Bradford, Dundee, Leicester, Nottingham and Wolverhampton etc
Skills and Enterprise Network – teleworking brief
Southwark Employment Unit – homeworking project
Greenwich Homeworkers project – independent community project
Warwickshire Rural Enterprise Network Telecottage
Wiltshire Telecottages Ltd

References and contacts

Acorn Televillage – Perton Farm, Stoke Edith, Hereford HR1 4HP Tel: 0432 899 0271

Bisset, L & Huws, U – *Sweated Labour: homeworking in Britain today*, Low Pay Unit, 1984

Department of Trade and Industry – *DTI Teleworking Study: summary of conclusions and recommendations*, DTI/MTA/Braemur, 1992

Employment Department, *Teleworking in Britain*, 1993
Huws, U – *Teleworking in Britain: A report to the Employment Department*, Research Series no 18, 1993
Huws, U – *No Sweat!*, National Group on Homeworking/TUC, 1996
Institute of Manpower Studies – *Flexibility for a few*, 1991
National Association of Teleworkers – Deerpark Telecentre, Honiton, Devon EX14 0PG
National Computing Centre Survey, 1992
National Group on Homeworking, Office 26, 30-38 Dock Street, Leeds LS10 1JF Tel: 0113 245 4273
Ownbase, 66 First Avenue, Bush Hill Park, Enfield EN1 1B
Telecottage Association, Stoneleigh Park, Warwickshire CV5 2R
Teleworking Association – The Other Cottage, Shortwood, Nailsworth, GL6 0SH

GLOSSARY

Automated call distribution (ACD):	computers used in call centres to distribute calls among call centre operators and which generate statistics – enabling monitoring such as average length of the call, time before calls are answered, number of calls abandoned, etc.
Audio conferencing:	using telephone systems simultaneously to connect employees working at different locations for virtual meetings
Bandwidth:	the amount of information that can flow through a given point at a given time; narrow bandwidth equals small amounts of information at a given time, whereas high bandwidth permits large amounts of information to flow through at one time
Baud rates:	the measurement of the speed of a modem
Call centres:	departments which exist for the sole purpose of dealing with inbound telephone communications and/or outbound calls. Generally, call centres use automated call distribution systems (ACD) to distribute calls among operators and use relevant customer information such as computerised customer records
Computer supported co-operative working (CSCW):	software tools and management techniques which facilitate the team working of

employees from different remote locations by computer. Examples include electronic mail, electronic diaries, software for tracking updates on a single document by several users and video conferencing tools such as the instant fax

Computer telephony integration (CTI): computerised technology, often used in call centres, to integrate computer held information on databases with telephone systems. For example, caller line identification codes can be used by CTI systems to identify the caller immediately on receipt of the call and to rapidly display the callers' customer records for the call centre operator

E-mail: electronic transmission of messages via the internet or organisational intranets

Fax card: a card, typically about the size of a credit card, which is inserted into a PC and connects the PC to the telephone line to provide faxing facilities directly from the PC

Fax modem: a modem integral to which is the relevant hardware and software for faxing documents

Groupware: comprises the various types of software, such as Lotus Notes, which enable workers to post information and to share it in a structured form both within and external to their organisations using intranet type technologies as the basis

Hypertext mark up language (HTML): a structured language used to generate hypertext pages for subsequent display on networks such as the world wide web

Hypertext: electronic text pages which contain active areas linked to other pages. The user is

	immediately transported to other pages of hypertext by clicking on the active area. This obviates the need for people to read pages of text sequentially
Internet:	the global network of computer networks enabling a user to send electronic messages and files. There are 40 million plus users worldwide. The internet has no single owner and is not centrally planned and controlled
Internet phones:	the facility whereby the internet is able to carry voice traffic at very little cost to anywhere in the world. Currently Internet phones have poor sound quality and there are concerns that they may slow down the internet because of the volume of data
Integrated services digital network (ISDN):	fibre optic telephone lines which allow up to 8 different devices to share one line. ISDN allows fast file transfer, video conferencing, high quality audio and faxing
Local area networks (LANs):	PCs which are connected together on a network to enable the PCs to access common software packages, share printers and store files
Modem:	an abbreviation of modulator/ demodulator. An electronic device for connecting a PC to a telephone line to enable the transfer or receipt of data
Optical character recognition (OCR):	software used with scanning devices which reads the typescript into the PC's software for subsequent editing
Portable document format:	a data format developed by Adobe which allows the reading of documents on different types of PC irrespective of the PC's operating system, fonts, etc.

Telecentres: centres ranging from simple, small neighbourhood offices to complex centres employing hundreds of people

Telecommuting: the practice of working at home or 'in transit' using PCs and telecommunications equipment

Teleworking: working at a distance from an employer and communicating with the centre, customer and other colleagues via PC, fax, telephone, etc.

Uniform resource locator (URL): a unique identifier, comparable to a map reference, for a site on the internet. The most frequently used URLs are those associated with the world wide web which always start with http://www

User ID: a name which identifies a user to a computer when the user connects

Video conferencing: the use of video telephony to show the image of the caller as well as the sound communication. This can range from one to one calls using inexpensive equipment to full scale high quality video conferencing suites with the ability to connect many people together at different locations

World Wide Web: an interface for users which gives access to the internet. The world wide web enables users to browse through different information held anywhere on the internet

References

Publications

1. *Teleworking Explained*: BT (1993)

2. *Teleworking in Britain*: UK Employment Department Report (1993)

3. *TeleFutures: A Study on Teleworking in Ireland:* (1996)

4. *The Social Implications of Teleworking*: The European Foundation for the Improvement of Living and Working Conditions (1996)

5. *Europe and Information Society*: Spikes, Cavell and Co. on behalf of 3Com Europe (1995)

6. *European Guide to Teleworking*: The European Foundation for the Improvement of Living and Working Conditions (1995)

7. *Employment and Economic Impacts of Advanced Communications, and Social Trends in Use of Communications Services*: DG XIII B, European Commission (1995)

8. *Legal, Organisational and Management Issues in Telework*: DG XIII B, European Commission (1995)

9. *Telework, Telecommuting and Decentralisation*: DG XIII B, European Commission (1995)

10. *Transport Statistics Report:* Department of Transport (1995)

11. *Working at a Distance – UK Teleworking and its Implications*: Parliamentary Office of Science and Technology, Houses of Parliament (1995)

12. *Teleworking – Right for Your Business, Right for Your People*: BT (1994)

13. *Teleworking – BT's Inverness Experience*: BT (1993)

14. *The Best of Both Worlds*: Department of Employment (1992)

15. *Knowledge Brokers Mobile Working Case Studies:* Knowledge Brokers (1996)

16. *Managing Teleworking*: BT Laboratories

17. *A Glimpse of the Future*: BT Laboratories

18. *Working at Home – A study of homeworking and teleworking*: Celia Stanworth Institute of Employment Rights (1996)

19. *Review of Telework in Britain: implications for public policy*: Gillespie et al, Newcastle University (1995)

20. *What new ways of working are made possible by technology?:* OTR (1996)

Professional magazines and articles

1. *European Journal of Teleworking*

2. *Telecommuting Review*

3. *Teleworker Magazine*

4. 'The 21st Century is Already on the Line', *The Times*, 14 August 1996

5. 'Work at Home? The Dream Hasn't Come True', Robert Uhlig, *Electronic Telegraph*, 26 October 1996

6. 'Europe and the Global Information Society', *The Bangemann Report*, 26 May 1994

7. 'Are We Being Run Over by the Virtual Office Bandwagon?', *Telecommuting Review*, 1994

8. ‘What’s ‘Real’ About Corporate Real Estate?’, *Telecommuting Review*, September 1994

9. ‘Death of a Giant: New Kinds of Working Toll the Death Knell for Big Office Blocks’, David Lawson, *Financial Times*, 1995